FINANCIAL SUPPORT FOR STUDENTS

Bedford Way Series
Published by Kogan Page in association with the Institute of Education, University of London

Financial Support for Students: grants, loans or graduate tax? Maureen Woodhall (ed.) *Personal and Social Education: philosophical perspectives* Patricia White (ed.) *Public Accountability and Quality Control in Higher Education* Cari P J Loder (ed.) *Reforming Religious Education: the religious clauses of the 1988 Education Reform Act* Edwin Cox and Josephine M Cairns.

THE BEDFORD WAY SERIES

8 .99

FINANCIAL SUPPORT FOR STUDENTS

Grants, Loans or Graduate Tax?

EDITED BY

MAUREEN WOODHALL

Contributors:
Nicholas Barr, Janet Hansen, Bruce Johnstone, Martin Morris,
Maureen Woodhall

KOGAN PAGE
Published in association with
The Institute of Education, University of London

First published in 1989 by Kogan Page Ltd.,
120 Pentonville Road, London N1 9JN

Printed and bound in Great Britain by Biddles Ltd, Guildford

British Library Cataloguing in Publication Data

Financial support for students : grants, loans or graduate tax. – (Bedford Way papers; ISSN 0261-0078;34)
   1. Higher education institutions. Students. Financial assistance
   I. Woodhall, Maureen II. Series
   378'.3

ISBN 1-85091-889-9

Contents

Notes on Contributors

Nicholas Barr is Senior Lecturer in Economics at the London School of Economics. With John Barnes he has written *Strategies for Higher Education: the alternative White Paper* (Aberdeen University Press, 1988) in which he proposes a new system of student loans in the United Kingdom. These proposals are reprinted in this book.

Janet Hansen is Director for Policy Analysis in the Washington office of the College Board, a non-profit-making organization in the United States that provides educational services for its membership, which includes more than 2,500 colleges, universities and higher education institutions and associations. She has written a number of books and articles on student aid, including *Student Loans: are they overburdening a generation?* (College Board, 1987).

Bruce Johnstone is Chancellor of the State University of New York, and was previously President of the State University of New York at Buffalo. In 1986 he carried out a comparative study of student financial assistance in five countries: the United Kingdom, the Federal Republic of Germany, France, Sweden and the United States. His book *Sharing the Costs of Higher Education* (College Board, 1986) is summarized in his chapter in this book.

Martin Morris was formerly Head of the Department of Biological Sciences, City of London Polytechnic. He carried out research on student loans in Sweden for his dissertation for the MA in Higher and Further Education at the Institute of Education in 1988. His chapter provides a summary of this research.

Maureen Woodhall is Senior Lecturer in Higher Education Finance at the Institute of Education, University of London. She has published widely on student support, including a study of student aid in Organization for Economic Co-operation and Development countries (OECD, 1978), *Student Loans: lessons from international experience* (Policy Studies Institute, 1982), *Student Loans as a Means of Financing Higher Education* (World Bank, 1983) and *Lending for Learning: designing a student loan programme for developing countries*

(Commonwealth Secretariat, 1987).

Gareth Williams, who contributes the Foreword, is Professor of Educational Administration at the Institute of Education, University of London.

Foreword
Gareth Williams

Everywhere the funding of higher education is under review. Old assumptions are being called into question. No longer is it being taken for granted that free higher education is necessarily cheap higher education, or good higher education, or efficient higher education, or equitable higher education. On the other hand, there are clearly problems in treating higher education simply as a commercial service, to be bought by individuals who think they will like it or profit from it. In most countries of the western world students are now expected to make some contribution to their living costs while they are studying and, in an increasing number, students are being expected to contribute to their tuition costs as well. The basic problem of financial support for students is easily stated. Most families are not in a position to pay the very considerable cost of higher education and many are unable or unwilling to pay the maintenance costs of continued study of offspring who are legally defined as adults. On the other hand, there is overwhelming evidence that for most students their higher education is a profitable private investment, yielding real economic returns that are well above those available from most other long-term investments.

If students are subsidized out of general taxation, this increases equity and efficiency to the extent that more people are able to benefit from higher education than would otherwise be the case. It is, however, inequitable from the point of view of those who are paying taxes but not able to undertake higher education. Furthermore, it is economically inefficient if higher education is subsidized but other long-term investments with equal potential rates of return are not.

In principle, students could borrow on the private money market to subsidize their studies. However, although the average return is good, the risks for any individual are quite high and banks have no effective collateral for what need to be quite substantial loans.

Considerations like these have led most governments to develop over the last quarter century schemes of financial support which combine some private contribution, some grant from public funds and some repayable loan.

The United Kingdom is unique in the extent to which students have been grant-supported out of public funds. However, the government has now made explicit proposals in its November 1988 White Paper to introduce a scheme which would by the early years of the next century result in repayable loans accounting for about half the financial support available to students. The decision to introduce a loan scheme after many years of discussion marks the beginning of a new stage of the debate, not the end of it. Once the principle of loans has been established there remain an enormous number of practical questions. These include:

- What proportion of support should be in the form of loans?
- Should interest payments be subsidized?
- What should be the position of graduates who cannot afford to repay their loans without considerable hardship?
- Should loans cover fees as well as maintenance costs?
- Should eligibility for loans be means-tested?
- Should a loans scheme be administered by the banks or by the government directly?
- Should the higher education institutions have a role in administering the scheme?

There is a wide variety of experience on all these issues in Western Europe, the United States and Japan. The aim of this volume is to open a new stage of the loans debate by examining some of the important practical aspects of the student loans issue in other Organization for Economic Co-operation and Development (OECD) countries. The papers have been assembled by Maureen Woodhall, who is the country's leading expert on student loans and who has written several books on the subject. She herself has contributed a wide-ranging introduction and summary of the issues involved.

Preface

The question of student support is likely to remain on the agenda in many countries in the 1990s as a number of changes are introduced into the existing student aid systems. It was in order to clarify the debate, which in the United Kingdom has for too long been narrowly confined to the question of whether students should receive grants or loans, that we decided, in the Centre for Higher Education Studies, to hold a one-day conference, in September 1988, to look at international experience with different types of student support, and to examine recent proposals for new kinds of loan, graduate tax, or other methods of student or graduate contribution. This book includes the papers presented at the conference, together with an analysis of the government's proposals for 'top-up' loans in the light of this international experience.

I am grateful to all our speakers for their contributions. I was very glad that Bruce Johnstone agreed to introduce the subject, by sharing with us his conclusions from a comparison of how costs of higher education are shared in five developed countries. I first met Bruce in the 1970s when he directed a study for the Ford Foundation on income-contingent loans and other types of student loan. We have shared an interest in international comparisons of student aid policy since that time, and I was delighted that he was able to speak at our conference, particularly since his recent appointment as Chancellor of the State University of New York means that he has an extremely busy schedule.

I was also delighted that Janet Hansen of the College Board was able to speak about American experience of student aid. As Director for Policy Analysis in the Washington office of the College Board, she has been extremely active in the student aid policy area for some years, and I was glad to have this opportunity to draw on the accumulated experience of the College Board in this area. I am also grateful to the College Board for permission to publish extracts from Bruce Johnstone's book, *Sharing the Costs of Higher Education*, which the Board commissioned and published in 1986.

I am grateful to the Aberdeen University Press for permission to reproduce part of John Barnes and Nicholas Barr's book, *Strategies for Higher Education*, which was published in October 1988 by

Aberdeen University Press for the David Hume Institute and the Suntory-Toyota International Centre for Economics and Related Disciplines at the London School of Economics. I should also like to thank Martin Morris for his contribution on Sweden. His paper for the conference was based on his dissertation for the MA in Higher and Further Education, which he completed in 1988 at the Centre for Higher Education Studies in the Institute of Education.

Finally, I must thank the participants in the conference for their lively and stimulating discussion, and Professor Gareth Williams who took the chair. I hope I have done justice to the wide ranging discussions that took place. I am grateful to all those who have helped to keep me informed about recent developments in the world of student support. I am responsible for any errors that remain in the book.

Chapter One
Introduction: Sharing the Costs of Higher Education
Maureen Woodhall

The purpose of this book

The early 1990s will be a time of major change in higher education in many countries. Demographic trends mean that universities, polytechnics and colleges throughout Europe and North America will be facing the problem of declining numbers of school leavers at a time when demand for graduates in the labour market will be growing. However, at the same time, financial pressures on higher education will continue or even increase, as governments seek to control or reduce public expenditure while responding to new claims on the public purse.

During the 1980s there have been significant changes in the level and mechanisms of funding higher education institutions in many countries. Not only in the United Kingdom, but in several other countries, the level of public support for higher education has been reduced, and institutions have been encouraged or forced by economic pressures to seek new sources of funds, for example from industrial and commercial sponsorship of research and continuing education and training. These trends are likely to continue; the funding of higher education institutions and the balance between public and private finance for teaching and research will remain a subject of political debate in many countries.

An equally urgent question that is now high on the political agenda, not only in the United Kingdom, but in several European countries, in the United States and in Australia and New Zealand, is how much and what type of financial support should governments provide for students in higher education. Major changes in systems of student financial assistance are being proposed or introduced in several countries. 1990 will see the introduction of student loans in the United

1

Kingdom, and at the same time there will be significant changes in Australia, Sweden and the Federal Republic of Germany in systems of student support, in the balance between grants and loans and the way in which graduates are required to contribute to the costs of higher education, by loan repayments or graduate tax. In the US the Higher Education Act will expire in 1991, and there will therefore be major debates over reauthorization of student aid programmes.

The next few years will therefore be a time of change, controversy and debate about financial support for students. Not since the mid 1960s, when signficant new programmes of student support were first introduced in many countries, has there been such widespread concern about whether students should receive grants, loans or pay a graduate tax, how the costs of higher education should be shared between students, parents and the taxpayer, and the effects of any solutions on participation in higher education. The effects of student aid on access, particularly by low-income students, women, ethnic minorities and mature students is of major concern when the number of eighteen year olds is declining in most developed countries. But other questions are equally pressing. What is the effect of rising burdens of debt in countries which already rely heavily on student loans? Do the problems of default, or high costs of administration or interest subsidies, wipe out any possible benefits from introducing or increasing loans? How much should parents be expected to contribute, or should students be encouraged to be financially independent? Should employers be required to make a more direct contribution to the costs of producing the skills and knowledge that they require from their graduate employees?

All these questions are being widely debated, and different countries are producing different solutions, and experimenting with new mechanisms for sharing the financial burdens of investing in tomorrow's workforce. It therefore seems opportune to examine international experience with grants, loans and other means of student support. No country is satisfied that it has yet developed a completely adequate system of student support, and the search continues for the best way of sharing the costs of higher education.

What common trends or problems have emerged during the 1980s and what lessons can be learned from international experience to guide decisions for the 1990s? It is in the hope of answering these questions that this book analyses recent trends in Australia, the Federal Republic of Germany, Sweden and the United States, and examines the UK government's proposals for student loans.

Not only is international experience very relevant to the current debate in the United Kingdom; it was in fact used to support the case for the introduction of student loans. An annex to the government White Paper on student loans (Department of Education and Science, 1988), which draws on Bruce Johnstone's research summarized in Chapter 2, presents a summary of student support in 12 countries. The White Paper argues that:

> The survey of other countries' arrangements highlights the availability of a greater variety of public support towards students' living costs, particularly in the USA. It is also notable that in those cases where provision is made mainly or entirely through grants, a relatively small proportion of students has access to it. Where loans are available as well as grants, the support generally extends to a large proportion of students. Britain is unique in attempting to support a large proportion of students with a grant. (ibid. p. 10).

Since this was published in November 1988, Kenneth Baker has argued on several occasions, mostly notably in a speech at Lancaster in January 1989, that a move towards an American-type system of student support, based on loans as well as grants, would allow an increase in the proportion of the population able to benefit from higher education. The American experience, summarized in Janet Hansen's paper in Chapter 3, is therefore particularly relevant to the current debate about student loans in Britain, and the likely effects on access.

American and other international experience is examined in some detail in this book. First, however, this introductory chapter gives a brief summary of the government proposals for student loans in the United Kingdom, and some of the alternative proposals put forward in recent months, and looks at some of the main issues that should be addressed in evaluating alternative systems or proposals for student support. These issues were discussed at a conference organized by the Centre for Higher Education Studies in September 1988. This discussion is summarized later in this chapter, together with some lessons from international experience which should be remembered when evaluating and monitoring the effects of the new student loan system in the years ahead.

The government's proposals
The White Paper, proposing 'top-up loans' for students was published in November 1988 (Department of Education and Science, 1988). The government proposed to introduce a top-up loan scheme, for the

academic year 1990-91 which would provide all full-time students in higher education with loans on the following terms:

- zero real interest
- no means-testing
- repayments responsive to earnings
- no cross-liability of spouses.

The purpose of these loans will be to top up the existing grant and parental contribution, but the intention is that as inflation reduces the real value of the current rates of grant and parental contribution, the real value of the loan will increase, until it represents half the total student support. On the assumption of an annual rate of inflation of 3 per cent, this point would be reached by 2007/8, as Figure 1 shows. However, if, as now seems increasingly likely, the rate of inflation remains above 3 per cent a year, loans would represent half the total student support before the year 2007.

Figure 1.1. Levels of grant, contribution and loan (1990-91 prices).

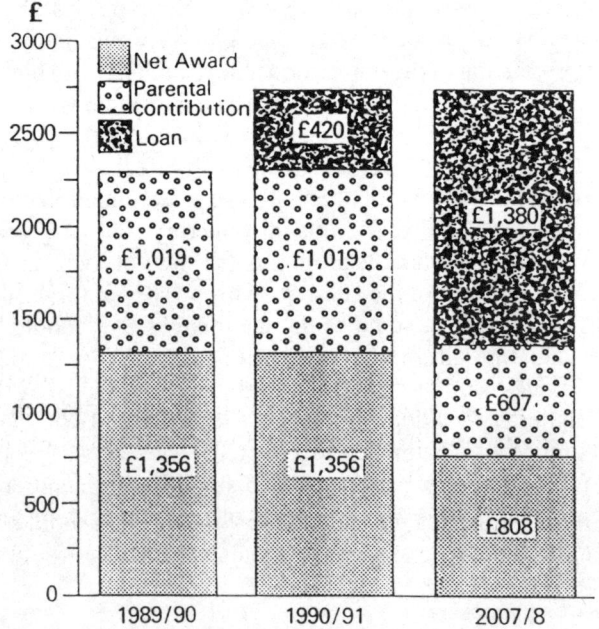

Figures apply to students with average parental contribution and award for 1990-91. The gross award is equivalent to the rate of grant payable outside London plus average additional allowance of £145.

Source: Department of Education and Science (1988, p.15).

Loans will be offered to all full-time students in higher education, up to the age of 50, and neither the student's own income, nor that of his or her parents or spouse will be taken into account in determining eligibility or size of the loan.

Repayment of the loan will start nine months after graduation and the debt will be revalued each year, in line with inflation, but no interest will be charged. The government proposes that repayments should be responsive to individuals' economic circumstances' (ibid. p.16) to ensure that decisions about choice of career or interruption of work to raise children 'should not be inhibited by an obligation to complete repayment of the loan'.

No precise details have yet been agreed, and the White Paper considers four possible repayment schemes:

1. The repayment term could be a fixed number of years, with the provision that in any year when earnings were low – for example less than 85 per cent of national average income – repayments could be deferred and the repayment period extended.
2. The repayment could be variable, with the annual instalment fixed, for example at £400 a year.
3. The repayment period could be fixed in line with the size of debt, so that those with large loans would have longer to repay.
4. Repayment could be directly related to taxable income, with the annual instalment expressed as a proportion of taxable income – perhaps in the region of 4 per cent – rather than a fixed sum. This would mean that any graduate with income below the income-tax threshold would automatically defer repayment, and the proportional burden of repayment for all those above this threshold would be the same, so that those with high earnings would repay their debt more quickly than those with a low income: 'The government expects that a student taking out a small loan and then earning an average graduate salary would complete repayments in five years. Graduates with large loans or lower earnings would take longer.' (ibid. p. 17).

The government 'does not intend that repaying the loan should be a lifelong commitment'. The circumstances under which a debt would be written off include:

- death
- either when the graduate reaches the age of 50, or 25 years after the loan commenced, whichever is sooner.

In addition to introducing top-up loans, the government intends to establish three access funds, to be administered by higher education institutions in order to provide discretionary bursaries. Each access fund will consist of £5 million a year to provide additional support to home students 'in cases where access to higher education might be inhibited by financial considerations or where students, for whatever reasons face real financial difficulties'. (ibid.p.18). The three funds are intended for:

1. Students in full-time higher education who are eligible for loans, whether or not they have a mandatory award.
2. Postgraduate students, who are not eligible for loans.
3. Students in full-time further education.

Once the loan scheme and discretionary bursary funds have been established, students will no longer be eligible for income support under the social security system, nor for unemployment benefit or housing benefit. The government estimates that this will save £65 million a year (in 1990 prices), compared with an initial expenditure on loans of £167 million. Thus, the White Paper proposals involve a net increase in public expenditure of about £120 million in 1990. Loan repayments will not generate any signficant savings for some years, but as the real value of the grant falls and loan repayments increase the government estimates that loan repayments will begin to cover the additional costs of providing top-up loans and discretionary bursaries by about 2001, and by 2018 there should be an annual saving in public expenditure of about £200 million (in 1990 prices).

These calculations are based on assumptions about increases in participation in higher education, the take-up of loans by students, inflation, the employment prospects of graduates and the proportion of graduates who defer repayment or default. The calculations do not take account of the costs of administering the loans, nor of any reduction in the costs of administering grants and social security benefits for students.

The White Paper does not explain how the loans will be administered, but states that the DES is discussing with banks, building societies and others, the arrangements for making loans and collecting repayments. 'The Government's objective is to identify a cost-effective scheme which the financial institutions will administer'. (ibid. p. 21). However, in the months following publication of the White Paper all the evidence in the press was that the banks remain unenthusiastic about the possibility of administering the loans, and no final announcement has yet been made.

Alternative proposals for loans in the UK

The White Paper states that 'there is scope for discussion about the way the loan scheme should be structured so as to provide students most effectively with the support they need' (ibid.p.21). Comments were invited on the desirable structure of the loans regime, particularly on the four options for repayment. Altogether over 100 submissions were sent to the Department of Education and Science (DES). It is likely that many of these would involve criticisms of the whole notion of top-up loans, but the White Paper made clear that:

> The government is convinced that the availability of a loan facility to top up the maintenance grant will provide a valuable extension of the sources of support available to students. It will support the broadening of participation in higher education, at the same time as sharing the cost of supporting students' maintenance more equitably between taxpayers, students' families and students themselves. (ibid.).

Thus, the question is not *whether* loans will be introduced, but *how* and on what terms. Various proposals have been made that would represent radical, rather than marginal, changes to the government's proposals.

Nicholas Barr has proposed a system of loans based on National Insurance Contributions (NICs), as he first proposed in the 'Alternative White Paper' (Barnes and Barr, 1988) and which he outlines in Chapter 6 of this book. Since the White Paper was published, he has elaborated on his proposals and compared them with the government's proposals for top-up loans (Barr, 1989).

He argues that a system of 'mortgage-type' loans, under which students borrow from public funds, but banks are responsible for both loan disbursements and the collection of loan repayments, would result in 'an administrative system of considerable complexity and huge cost'. His estimates of the administrative cost of the scheme, together with the cost of interest subsidy implied by the government's proposal to offer loans at zero real interest rates, lead Barr to the conclusion that the White Paper scheme would actually increase the Public Sector Borrowing Requirement (PSBR) by £300 million by 2005 and by £175 million in the long run. On the other hand, he estimates that a system of loans with income-related repayment, collected by employers by an additional NIC payable by graduates, would reduce the PSBR by £300 million in 2005 and by £350 million in the long run. He believes the reasons for this enormous difference are firstly that default and write-off of loans, 'leakage', would be much less under an NIC-based system than under a system of mortgage-type loans, with repayments collected by the banks; secondly, there would be no need for interest subsidies; and thirdly that start-up funds for such a scheme could come from the private sector, rather than from the public funds.

Thus Barr argues that a scheme of student loans with repayment based on National Insurance contributions is simultaneously

> fair, efficient, cheap, administratively simple, easy to understand, flexible and politically attractive. It would have a major impact on access and expansion. It could be put in place immediately. (Barr 1989).

Barr's proposal has been widely discussed, but there has been no official reaction to his argument that an NIC-based scheme would offer many advantages over the White Paper proposals.

The idea of income-related contributions, possibly linked to NICs has, however, been taken up by others including, most significantly, the Committee of Vice-Chancellors and Principals (CVCP). In its response to the White Paper (CVCP, 1989) the Committee proposed a 'graduate tax contribution' rather than a loan scheme, but argued that these contributions could be paid through either the tax or the National Insurance system. The CVCP announced, in its original submission to the DES review of student support in 1986, the criteria it believed that any new system of student support should meet. These are that the scheme should:

- be *simple*
- provide students with *adequate* support while they study
- provide students with *certainty* that they will receive this support
- satisfy the requirements of *social justice*.

The CVCP believes that the proposed top-up loans do not meet these criteria, and instead proposes that all graduates should be required to pay income-related contributions, over a period of, say, ten years; these contributions could be collected via income tax or NICs. The CVCP argues that

> if the principle of a 'graduate contribution' were accepted there would be a strong case for restoring the real value of the grant, taking account of regional differences, abolishing the parental contribution and eliminating the means test. Together, they would satisfy the Committee's

criteria by being adequate, simple, certain and socially just, in a way that the government proposals are not. (ibid.)

Others have followed Barnes and Barr in taking up the idea of income-related contributions or loan repayments, and linking this proposal with the idea of a significant increase in tuition fees for all home students, possibly even full-cost fees, to be paid by a combinations of state bursary or higher education voucher, supplemented by loans. Some of these proposals could lead to loans which were more substantial than the top-up facility envisaged in the White Paper.

What evidence is there from other countries, about whether student loans, with or without income-related repayment, or some other form of 'graduate contribution' would meet the criteria of simplicity, adequacy, certainty and social justice? That is the subject of the chapters that follow, and the remainder of this chapter provides a brief summary of the evidence, the issues it raises, and the lessons for Britain.

The evidence from other countries: a summary

A comparative perspective on sharing the costs of higher education has been provided by Bruce Johnstone who carried out a comparative analysis of student support systems in 1985-86 in the United States of America, the Federal Republic of Germany, France, Sweden and the United Kingdom (Johnstone, 1986). He has summed up his conclusions as follows:

> One of the happy outcomes of international comparative studies is the comforting realization that we are not alone whether in our goals, our problems, or often times even in our selection of solutions. But another advantage, every bit as useful, is the realization that there are often other, very different, ways of doing things. For example, nations vary in the way the costs of higher education are shared among parents, students, taxpayers and institutions. (Johnstone, 1987, p. 89)

This comparative analysis is summarized in Chapter 2 'International Comparisons of Student Financial Support'. Johnstone warns that 'the solutions formed by one country are rarely transportable intact to another', and his conclusion is that there is no single system of student financial support that satisfies all the many varied objectives of student aid programmes:

> The judgement as to which country's system is best depends on an individual's circumstances:

- If you are a very good, full-time student, you would do well to be British. You would get free tuition and $3500 to $4000 for studying in London, with no self-help expectations.
- If you are academically weak or a part-time or an otherwise non-traditioal student, you would do well to be American. Higher education is highly accessible, tuitions are low (if not zero) in the public sector, part-time students are eligible for some grant aid, and term-time work and loans are abundant.
- If you are a parent, try to be Swedish. There is no expectations of parental support, regardless of your means or your children's choice of university. In a similar vein, if you are a married adult whose spouse aspires to higher education, you should also be a citizen of Sweden, where you will have no financial responsibility for your mate's costs of tuition or living.
- If you are going to have to borrow, try to be German. You will have five years of grace after graduation and then up to 20 years to repay at zero per cent interest, with additional bonuses if you finish early or in the top 30 per cent of your class.
- If you are a taxpayer, from the standpoint of minimizing your burden of higher educational expenses you had best be French. The tax-supported, per-student operating expenses of the universities are low (at least by Northern European and North American standards), the grant aid to students is minuscule, and parents must be terribly poor to qualify for any assistance anyway. (Johnstone, 1987, pp. 91-2).

The American experience is examined in more detail in Chapter 3 by Janet Hansen, author of a number of studies of student aid policy in the United States, including a recent study of student debt burdens commissioned by the joint Economic Committee of the US Congress (Hansen, 1987). Janet Hansen provides an overview of 'Cost-Sharing in Higher Education: the United States Experience', which summarizes American student aid policy since the first student loan programme was introduced by the federal government in 1958. She also gives an authoritative summary of recent evidence on such issues as default, debt burdens and the cost to the federal government of interest subsidies and the 'special allowance' paid to the commercial banks which administer student loans. Her chapter also draws a number of general conclusions which are extremely relevant to the current debate in Britain and elsewhere on student aid policy, particularly on whether student loan schemes can work successfully.

One answer to this question is provided by the statistics of student aid in the US. In 1987-88 four million American students and their parents borrowed a total of $12 billion to pay for higher education.

Janet Hansen shows how the total valume of student loans has risen dramatically, from $1.2 billion in 1970 to over $12 billion today. She examines the implications of this growth, and looks at the costs and benefits of student loans, both from the point of view of taxpayers and student borrowers. Her general conclusions are that 'burden-sharing among parents, students, taxpayers and institutions/philanthropists works, at least in our context' and that 'up to a point, student loans increase the financial resources available to pay for college, without deleterious effects on borrowers'.(P.65).

However, Americans continue to debate the strengths and weaknesses of student loans and other types of student support, as the new Congress prepares to consider the reauthorization of the Higher Education Act. Early in 1989, the College Board published a review of student-loan policy alternatives facing the US federal government, which asked whether it was time for *Radical Reform or Incremental Change?* (Gladieux, 1989).

These proposals, and proposals for change in other countries, including Australia and New Zealand and the Federal Republic of Germany, are examined in Chapter 4, 'International Experience of Financial Support for Students: Recent Trends and Developments'.

The trend which Janet Hansen identifies, in the United States, of increased reliance on student loans and a policy in the 1980s of shifting financial burdens from taxpayers to students and their parents, particularly those from middle- or upper-income families, is not a uniquely American phenomenon. Not only have the Reagan administration in the US and the Conservative government in Britain attempted to reduce the burden on taxpayers by reducing the real value of grants to students, and increasing loans (in the US) or introducing them (in the UK, from 1990), but in other countries also, including the Federal Republic of Germany and Japan, there has been increased reliance on student loans in the 1980s. Recently both the Australian and New Zealand governments have considered the introduction of student loans or a graduate tax, as part of a conscious policy of shifting financial burdens from taxpayers to those who directly benefit from higher education. The Committee on Higher Education Funding in Australia argued that

> The advantaged who use and benefit directly from higher education ought to contribute more directly to the cost of the system and Australian taxpayers should not be expected to carry the burden of financing the growth envisaged in higher education, particularly since few directly

enjoy its financial benefits. (Committee on Higher Education Funding, 1988)

Similarly, a committee in New Zealand recommended a system of loans repayble through the tax-system, and argued that 'the logic of the scheme is to secure a better balance of private and public costs with private and public benefits' (Hawke, 1988). In November 1988 the German Federal Republic government also published a report on the operation of the student support system (BAföG) (Der Bundesminister für Bildung und Wissenchaft, 1988) and changes in the German system may be announced later in 1989.

Sweden has provided a combination of grants and loans for students since 1965, and has, like the US and the Federal Republic of Germany, relied increasingly on loans until, in 1988, loans represented over 90 per cent of all financial support for students in higher education. The balance between grants and loans began to cause increasing concern in the 1980s and the Swedish government therefore set up a National Commission to review the student support system. As a result of its report major changes were introduced in January 1989. In Chapter 5, 'Student Aid in Sweden: Recent Experience and Reforms', Morris examines the criticisms that have been voiced in Sweden of the previous system, and compares the new system, introduced in 1989, with its predecessor. Some critics of student loans have seized upon the recent changes in Sweden as evidence that loans do not work, and that grants are preferable to loans. However, under the new system, loans will still represent 70 per cent of total student support for those in higher education, and the National Board of Student Aid, which administers both grants and loans, believes that, with the changes that have been introduced in 1989, the combined grant and loan system in Sweden will provide an adequate and equitable system of student support.

In Britain, on the other hand, the system of student support in the 1980s has been criticized as neither adequate nor equitable. Nicholas Barr summarizes these criticisms, presents his own proposals for a student loan programme in Britain, and compares these with other possible types of loan in Chapter 6, 'Alternative Proposals for Student Loans in the United Kingdom'.

These proposals, and the experiences of other countries with loans, provoked heated discussions at our conference but there was no consensus about the desirable balance between grants, loans and other types of student support. There was general recognition that some change in the British system of student support was inevitable and probably overdue but, just as in the US there is disagreement between the advocates of radical reform and those who favour incremental change, so at the conference there was a division of opinion between those who saw the necessity for a 'big bang' approach, which would introduce a major change, such as a graduate tax or Nicholas Barr's proposal for loans to be repaid through National Insurance contributions (NICs) and those who favoured a 'top-up' scheme, as the White Paper has proposed. The dicussion ranged far and wide and it became clear that evaluating different systems of student support raises a number of issues which are summarized in the following section.

Evaluating alternative systems of student support: the issues
Many of those who are persuaded that the introduction of loans could offer advantages in terms of increased flexibility, are worried about the effects on access for disadvantaged groups, particularly students from low-income families, ethnic minorities and women and mature students, whose increased participation in higher education could be threatened by a fear of loans. There is also concern about default rates, about the magnitude of debt burdens, particularly at a time of rising interest rates, and about the effects of student loans on the labour market, particularly at a time of rising demand for graduates coupled with declining numbers of eighteen-year-old school leavers.

There was considerable discussion about the mechanics of student loan programmes, for example whether loans should be provided by banks or by a government agency, how repayments should be collected, and what should be the role of universities, polytechnics, and other institutions, which under some systems have to bear part of the costs of administering loans, collecting repayments or advising students about the complexities of student aid. This section does not attempt a detailed record of all the conference discussions, but gives a summary of some of the main issues, under five broad heads:

1. The concept of 'cost sharing', and the widespread attempts, in many countries, to shift part of the burden of costs from the taxpayer to other partners.
2. The effects of loans on access to higher education, and in particular whether the introduction of loans in Britain could help to widen access, as the government has argued, or whether participation would be confined to the wealthy, as the National Union of

Students has long maintained.
3. Concerns about loan defaults and debt burdens.
4. Mechanisms for administration of loans and the collection of repayments.
5. The objectives of student support and in particular, the existance of trade-offs between different objectives, aims, or criteria when designing a student loan scheme, for example between flexibility and complexity, or between the desire to reduce public expenditure and the need to ensure the political acceptability of any new scheme.

Cost-sharing
Bruce Johnstone's framework for a comparative analysis of student support systems, in terms of the sharing of financial burdens between taxpayers, students, parents and other partners, including institutions and employers, helped to shape much of the discussion. In Chapter 2 Bruce Johnstone emphasizes that any attempt to change the financial burdens is a 'zero sum game': 'any cost shifted *from* one source must perforce be shifted *to* another'. In the discussion it was emphasized that while attemps to shift the relative *shares* borne by different partners represented a zero sum game the overall *amount* of expenditure on student support should not be regarded as pre-determined. Many participants argued strongly that changes in student support in Britain should be designed to encourage expansion of higher education opportunities, and not simply to redistribute financial burdens.

There was considerable disagreement about the desirability of maintaining the parental share of higher education costs. Both Bruce Johnstone and Janet Hansen stress that in the United States parents are expected to contribute to the costs of their children's higher education when they can afford to do so, and indeed one loan programme, Parent Loans for Undergraduate Study (PLUS loans) is explicitly designed to help parents meet that financial burden. Janet Hansen argues that 'all of the potential partners need to share the burdens of college financing if access to education is to grow'. Many Americans would share her conviction that the key to the very wide access to higher education in the US, is the fact that costs are also widely shared.

On the other hand, the fact that in the United Kingdom there is widespread evidence that many students do not receive the full 'parental contribution' that is assumed in their grant assessment leads many people to argue that the parental contribution should be abolished. Participants disagreed about whether an expected parental contribution is desirable, on grounds of equity, or should be phased out, as Nicholas Barr suggests, on the grounds that is is both inefficient and universally unpopular.

There was some discussion about the shares of other potential partners, in particular employers and institutions. Concern was expressed that if employers are required to contribute to the costs of higher education, for example through an increase in the NIC share contributions, as Nicholas Barr suggests, this would create a disincentive to employ graduates. Alternatively employers might simply pass on the cost to consumers as increased prices for goods and services produced by graduates, which would be inflationary.

There is also some concern about whether some of the costs of administering a student loan scheme might fall on the institutions, if they were required to help administer a loan programme, as is the case with Perkins Loans (formerly known as National Direct Student Loans) in the US, which are administered by the student financial aid offices on university and college campuses, or if they had to provide information to banks or other agencies providing student loans. In either case there is likely to be a demand for increased financial advice for students on the implications of loans and some of this burden is likely to fall on institutions at a time when administrative burdens are already increasing in universities and polytechnics as a result of other financial changes.

The main concern, however, was about the effects of attempts to shift part of the costs of higher education from the taxpayer to students, as has been proposed in Australia and now in Britain. This led, inevitably, to a discussion of the effects of loans on access.

Access

The main argument put forward against loans by the National Union of Students (NUS) and other prominent critics, is that they would discourage participation by low-income students and other disadvantaged groups, particularly ethnic minorities, women and mature students. Experience in Sweden and the US provides no evidence to support the argument that loans deter women and a graduate's loan debt will represent a 'negative dowry'. Janet Hansen points out in her paper that 'despite fears about creating negative dowries, loans have clearly not discouraged the enrolment of women, who now represent a majority of college students in the US'. Similarly,

Martin Morris shows that in Sweden the proportion of women in higher education has increased, rather than declined, since the introduction of student loans.

Nevertheless, there are fears that in the UK loans might deter women, and that they will represent a particular obstacle to woder participation by mature students. In the US, loans are available to mature students as well as school-leavers, and to part-time as well as fulll-time students. In the UK only full-time students are eligible for grants and many participants argued that any reform of student support should provide increased assistance for mature students, including those who wish to study part-time.

Participants were also concerned about the effects of loans on attempts to widen access by increasing participation of low-income students and ethnic minorities. Another aspect of access was emphasized by some participants who feared that loans would discourage students from studying away from home and this would discriminate against those living in remote regions with limited opportunities for higher eduation. It would also threaten the viability of some institutions with a very limited 'local' catchment area.

Loan defaults and debt burdens
Janet Hansen's chapter reports increased concern in the United States about rising levels of default and student indebtedness, although she points out that research in this area suggests that 'borrowing is not out of control and most student borrowers have quite manageable debt burdens' and also that

> while default costs have sky rocketed, the default *rate* has increased only a little. Our newly-discovered default 'problem' stems from the large increase in borrowing, leading to larger amounts of debt coming into repayment. It is not the result of a growing unwillingness to repay student loans.(p.62)

Nevertheless, participants were concerned about the dangers of default and about what constituted a 'manageable' burden of debt.

American evidence suggests that those who are most likely to default are not graduates with large debt burdens, but students who have dropped out of higher education, or those who took short, vocational programmes but subsequently failed to find jobs or have very low incomes. Thus schemes which allow those with low incomes to postpone repayment, as in Sweden, or which link repayment to income level, as in the new Australian scheme, are likely to minimize the danger of default. Nicholas Barr emphasizes in his chapter that income-related repayment, based on national insurance, would minimize default and prevent unfair debt burdens.

> Someone who is unemployed makes no repayments whilst he or she is unemployed, and a graduate nurse pays back very little, a least early in her career. Both features are crucial to the efficiency and equity, and also to the political acceptability, of any substantial reliance on loans. (p.118)

Thus, the question of default and what constitutes a 'manageable' burden of debt were seen to be closely linked with the mechanisms for administering loans and for collecting loan repayments.

Mechanisms for administration of loans and collection of repayments
There was no agreement about whether student loans should be administered by the banks, as in the case of Guaranteed Student Loans (GSL) and PLUS loans in the US; by institutions, as in the case of Perkins Loans in the US; or by a state agency or 'quango' as in Sweden. Clearly one important factor is the relative costs of different methods of administration. American experience shows that it is perfectly possible to devise a scheme which is attractive to the banks, but the cost to the taxpayer – in terms of the 'special allowance' which is paid to the banks to cover administrative costs – is high. Janet Hansen's chapter concludes that using private markets rather than a government agency to provide loan capital 'has pluses and minuses'.

Several participants felt that to collect loan repayments through tax or national insurance contributions would have cost advantages. However, the Inland Revenue's objections to becoming debt collectors rather than tax gatherers is well known, and the NIC scheme would also involve a fundamental change in a scheme designed to provide insurance against future risks of sickness and unemployment, rather than to collect payment for past participation in higher education. Nicholas Barr, on the other hand, argues that

> People already pay contributions for a future benefit like pensions; here they pay a contribution for a past benefit. The principle is entirely the same; in both cases national insurance enables an individual to redistribute income over his or her lifetime. (p. 119)

The objectives of student support
Much of the discussion focused on the objectives of student support. Both Bruce Johnstone and Janet Hansen stress that the complexity of the American system of student support derives from the fact that it is

trying to meet a number of different objectives, and Janet Hansen's chapter argues that 'one consequence of the evolutionary development of American student aid is that the goals of the system are murky'. She draws on a recent evaluation of student aid policy (McPherson, 1987) to suggest that federal student aid policy has three major purposes:

• equalizing educational opportunity;
• making the sharing of higher education's costs and benefits fairer;
• and making higher education institutions work better by making them financially more secure.(p.57)

In the UK, also, there is confusion about the objectives of student support, and the discussion emphasized that any proposals to change the existing system must be based on clear and unambiguous objectives. A scheme designed to widen access and increase participation in higher education will not save taxpayers' money. A scheme designed to reduce public expenditure will not increase participation. A scheme designed to reduce the burden of parental contributions must either involve an increase in the taxpayers' burden or a shift in the burden from parents to students. Everyone recognized the difficulty of reconciling the conflicting interests and objectives of the Treasury, with its concern over public expenditure, parents and students concerned about their own financial burdens, employers who argue that the future needs of the economy and the labour market require an expansion of higher education, and politicians concerned about the political acceptability of changes in student support and their effects on voters – who may be parents, students or employers. When we add to this list of competing interests and objectives the demands of social justice, that require equality of opportunity for higher education, as well as the demands for efficiency and equity in the sharing of cost, then it becomes clearer why there was no general agreement in the conference about either the objectives of student support or the best way of achieving them.

Participants disagreed about whether we need a system of 'top-up' loans, designed to fill acknowledged gaps in the present system, or a more radical change, designed to redistribute the costs of higher education. There was also disagreement about the priority of different types of gap. For example, one definition of 'top-up loans' would simply allow students who currently fail to get the full parental contribution to borrow to fill this gap. A more generous definition would allow students who are currently ineligible for a mandatory grant, because they are studying part time or taking a non-designated course of study, to take out a loan to fill this gap. Yet another definition would allow students to borrow to 'top-up' the declining value of maintenance grants, which have fallen by nearly 25 per cent in real terms since 1962.

Even if it were agreed that the main purpose of a system of 'top-up' loans should be to fill such gaps, there would still be the problem of deciding which gaps are the most serious. Some argued that a system designed simply to fill gaps would reveal much wider gaps than the government would be prepared to overcome, while others argued for more ambitious aims.

Another problem identified in Janet Hansen's chapter is the need to reconcile demands for simplicity and flexibility. On the basis of American experience, she draws the conclusion that 'in designing student aid programmes there is an important trade-off to consider between minimizing complexity of administration and maximizing flexibility in meeting student needs' (p. 65). There was some discussion of this trade-off in the British context, and broad agreement that a loan scheme should not be too complex, if it is to win wide acceptance.

In general, however, many participants believed that complexity should be avoided in designing a student support scheme. The discussions demonstrated the complexity of the policy issues raised in analysing alternative methods of student support. By the end of the conference participants understood more clearly why in Britain the publication of the government's proposals had been so long delayed or postponed, and why other countries are also continuing to debate changes in systems of student support.

Lessons from international experience
In the light of past experience with shifting some of the costs of higher education from students and parents to taxpayers, and recent attempts and proposals to shift part of this burden again, this time from taxpayers to students, what lessons can be drawn from international experience about the feasibility and the likely effects of students loans and other support?

First, it is clear that most, if not all, of the governments and the commentators considered here seem convinced that student support should include both an element of grant and a loan, or other student contribution, payable through the tax or national insurance system. There are still arguments about the precise balance between grants, loans or graduate tax, but there is widespread support for the belief that a mixture of grants and loans with some element of interest subsidy or low-income insurance, provides an equitable means of sharing financial burdens. Most, but not all, countries expect a parental contribution, but there is increasing recognition that a student contribution is also necessary, since students will derive substantial benefits from higher education. Thus, the White Paper's assertion that top-up loans, to supplement grants, will support the broadening of participation in higher education, at the same time as sharing the cost of supporting students' maintenance more equitably between taxpayers, students' families and students themselves is consistent with the experience of other countries reviewed here. Even a system of 50 per cent grant, 50 per cent loan, will be more generous than the new Swedish system, and it is what is being proposed now in the Federal Republic of Germany.

The terms of the proposed 'top-up' loans will be generous by American standards, with zero real interest rates and repayment spread over 25 years, if necessary. The fact that the loans will not be means-tested is also generous, in comparison with the USA, where eligibility for subsidized GSLs is determined by family income. The virtual abolition of means-testing in 1978 with the Middle Income Student Assistance Act (MISAA) proved very costly to the federal government, which now maintains tight control of eligibility for GSLs. As a result of MISAA demand for student loans in the USA grew very rapidly, as students, and their parents, realized that loans backed by government guarantee and a hefty subsidy were very attractive. Therefore Americans may now be wondering why middle-income students in Britain have not welcomed the proposed top-up loans, instead of protesting about them. American experience also suggests that the costs of administering the scheme, and of keeping defaults to a minimum, may be substantial. The banks here are trying to ensure that the government will subsidize the costs, as the US federal government does, and these costs, together with the interest subsidies to borrowers, will certainly mean that there will be no substantial saving of public funds when loans are introduced.

There seems to be no simple relationship between type of student support and level of participation in higher education. There is no evidence that loans necessarily discourage participation, or that grants are more likely to lead to high levels of participation. Indeed, the fact that the overall rate of participation in higher education is more than twice as high in the US, with its heavy reliance on loans, than in the UK, which up to now has provided only grants, and that women and mature students make up a much bigger proportion of the student total in the US than the UK, shows that the relationship between student support and levels of participation is more complex than many critics of loans have supposed.

It is clear that general economic and labour market conditions are often as important as methods of student support in determining the financial incentives to participate in higher education. When graduate job prospects and relative earnings are favourable, this leads to strong demand for higher education, and students will be willing to borrow to help finance that investment. This was demonstrated in both Sweden and the US when the introduction of student loans in the 1960s was accompanied by a strong labour market for graduates, and demand for higher education grew. When economic conditions changed, and when relative graduate salaries in Sweden declined, the demand for higher education stagnated, but this was judged to be mainly the result of general economic conditions rather than the effects of the student support system. Therefore several participants emphasized that it will be the state of the British economy in the 1990s, including the labour market for graduates and the level of inflation and interest rates, that determines attitudes to student loans, once they are introduced in 1990-91.

The evidence from abroad strongly supports the need for some kind of income-related repayment, whether by means of option D in the White Paper or by means of a tax- or NIC-repayment, as proposed by Nicholas Barr. By proposing that those with low incomes may defer repayment the White Paper deals with the problem of excessive debt burdens leading to high rates of default, and American and Swedish experience suggests that default need not be a major problem.

Finally, there is the question of the likely effects of loans on participation. Despite the three 'access' funds, there are still going to be many potential students who will not have access to financial support. Part-time students, or those whose parents will not pay their expected contribution, will not have the opportunity to borrow as they do in the US. On the other hand, American and Swedish experience does not suggest that women and mature students will be discouraged by loans. Thus, while top-up loans will not necessarily reduce access, as their critics maintain, there is no evidence that the system outlined in the White Paper will lead to a large-scale expansion of opportunities, as many people, including Kenneth Baker, say they want to see.

What is clear is that there must be very careful analysis of the effects of the new loans. The White Paper states that 'the DES will monitor the introduction of the new regime, so as to measure its effects on such matters as participation by social class or gender'. This book suggests that since major changes in student support will also be introduced or begin to operate in other countries in the 1990s, there will be a unique opportunity to analyse the effects of changes in student support from a comparative international perspective.

References

Barnes, J. and Barr, N. (1988), *Strategies for Higher Education: the alternative White Paper*. Aberdeen: Aberdeen University Press.

Barr, N. (1988), *Student Loans: the next steps*. Aberdeen: Aberdeen University Press.

Committee of Vice-Chancellors and Principals (CVCP) (1989), *Response of the Committee of Vice-Chancellors and Principals to the Government's White Paper 'Top-Up Loans for Students'*, mimeo and associated press-release, 7 February. London: CVCP.

Committee of Higher Education Funding (Australia) (1988), *Report of the Committee on Higher Education Funding*, Chairman, Neville Wran. Canberra: Australian Government Publishing Service.

Der Bundesminister für Bildung und Wissenschaft (1988), *Vorschlage zur Reform des Bundesausbildungsförderungsgesetzes (BAföG)*. Bonn: Herausgegeben vom Bundesminister für Bildung und Wissenschaft.

Department of Education and Science (1988), *Top-Up Loans for Students*. London: HMSO (Cm. 520).

Gladieux, L. (ed.) (1989), *Radical Reform or Incremental Change? Student loan policy alternatives for the Federal Government*. New York: College Entrance Examination Board.

Hansen, J. (1987), *Student Loans: are they overburdening a generation?* Washington DC: The College Board.

Hawke, G. R. (1988), *Report of the Working Group on Post Compulsory Education and Training* (Convenor: Professor G. R. Hawke). Wellington: Victoria University of Wellington.

Johnstone, B. (1986), *Sharing the Costs of Higher Education: student financial assistance in the UK, the Federal Republic of Germany, France, Sweden and the US*. New York: College Entrance Examination Board.

Johnstone, B. (1987), 'International perspectives: a five-nation study' in J. M. Cronin and S. Q. Simmons (eds.) (1987), *Student Loans: risks and realities*. Dover, Mass.: Auburn House Publishing, pp.89-103.

McPherson, M. (1987), *How Can We Tell if Federal Student Aid is Working?* New York: College Entrance Examination Board.

Chapter Two
International Comparisons of Student Financial Support
Bruce Johnstone

This chapter presents a summary of my book on the costs of higher education in five countries: the United States, the United Kingdom, the Federal Republic of Germany, France and Sweden (Johnstone, 1986). The book concentrates on the direct 'out-of-pocket' expenses that initially face students and their parents as they attempt to meet the costs of student living (room, board, books, travel and all other such expenses) plus whatever proportion of the costs of instruction may be passed on to them through tuition fees. More specifically, it is about the way those costs are ultimately borne by the parents, the student himself or herself, the taxpayer (a word that will generally be employed in preference to the more euphemistic 'government' or 'public'), and institutions or philanthropists.

It was a major premise of this study, borne out by the research, that countries must balance very similar public policy goals in apportioning these costs (e.g. equal higher educational opportunities, efficient use of public resources and equitable distribution of costs and benefits) and that each country can benefit in the refinement of its objectives and in the choice of its instruments (e.g. financial-need analysis, means-tested grants, student loan programmes) by understanding what countries with similar higher educational systems and public policy objectives are doing.

The sources of revenue
Regardless of the system, society or country, the costs of higher education must be shared by some combination of the following four sources of revenue: parents, students, taxpayers and institutions (i.e. colleges or universities which derive extra revenues from philanthropists or donors to help students).

Parents are expected in most, although not all, countries to contribute at least to the costs of student living. In the United States, they are also expected to contribute a portion of the instructional costs through the payment of tuition fees: a large portion at private institutions, which receive relatively little (in some cases, no) direct governmental, or taxpayer-borne, aid; and a relatively small portion at public colleges and universities, where tuition fees are lower. Parental contributions are limited by ability to pay – generally as measured by current income, sometimes also by wealth or assets, and usually modified by special considerations such as number of dependent children. Parental contributions may come from savings, from reduced current consumption or from borrowing against future earnings. Parental contributions may be through cash or 'in kind', particularly in the support of students living at home.

Students may pay a portion of the costs of student living and also, if tuition fees are charged, a portion of the instructional costs. Student-borne revenues may come from their own assets or savings, from term-time earnings, or from loans to be repaid from future earnings. Spouses, too, may be possible contributors to the costs of higher education and are treated for the purpose of this analysis as though their earnings were an extension of the students' own. Similarly, the unmarried partner (in France, the *conjoint*) may be a significant, though unofficial, source of support. At the same time, public policy in Scandinavia holds the working spouse not responsible for contributions to living costs of his or her student spouse – a principle that releases the student from dependence on his or her working spouse, but that necessarily places a somewhat greater burden on the student and the taxpayer.

Taxpayers in most European countries pay all or nearly all of the direct instructional costs plus some portion of the costs of student living. In the United States, the taxpayer pays most of the instructional costs in the public sector and a portion of those in the private sector, either through direct institutional grants or through payment of a portion of the tuition costs. The costs of a student living in the United States and in most European countries are supported by some combination of direct cash grants; loan-repayment subsidies (e.g. in the form of low interest rates or forgiveness of a portion of the principal amount borrowed); indirect subsidies of room, board and other expenses (e.g. as in some European countries, through government-subsidized canteens, low-cost housing or special travel fares); or by special tax advantages to the parents of students, which have the effect of shifting costs from taxpayers who happen to have children in college to taxpayers generally. Living costs are supported in most countries according to parental means, or 'need': that is, are reduced as parents' incomes increase and as the need for the taxpayer subsidy declines.

Institutions/Philanthropists in some countries may contribute to a portion of direct instructional costs through endowment income or current gifts applied to operations. They may also contribute to a portion of the costs of student living through grants or scholarships originating through endowments or current donations and most often given by the institution according to need. Institutional/philanthropic support is particularly prevalent in the United States, probably because of the tradition of the autonomous private institution. This has always required alumni support in order to survive and therefore assiduously cultivates the loyalty of alumni to their Alma Mater. In addition US tax laws very substantially reward donations to tax-exempt, non-proft-making corporations, thus reducing the real cost of giving and, in effect, shifting some of the ultimate burden of such gifts on to the general taxpayers, who must make up the lost revenue.

The costs of higher education and the distribution of these costs amoung the four sources of revenue, or 'bearers of the burden', are summarized in Table 2.1. It is a fundamental premise of this study that *all* the costs of higher education are borne by some combination of these four sources – regardless of system or nation – and that any cost shifted *from* one source must perforce be shifted *to* another.

Contributions from industry and business
Industry or business may also contribute to the costs of instruction, and occasionally to the costs of student living as well, through unrestricted gifts to colleges and universities or through tuition fees paid on behalf of employees or other recipients of business scholarships. Business gifts to higher education are much more significant in the United States than elsewhere. Even in the United States, however, much business giving to higher education is restricted and cannot be said to contribute significantly to covering the overall cost of undergraduate instruction.

But a much more serious qualification to the inclusion of business as a true partner in the bearing of college costs is the question of ultimate incidence. After all, only people, or institutions on behalf of people, not businesses or corporations themselves, own assets and ultimately derive (or forgo) income. When a business is said to make a contribution to a university, college or to an employee scholarship

Table 2.1. Costs of higher education and sources of revenue.

	Costs of higher education	
	Costs of education and living	*Costs of instruction*
Sources of revenue	• Room • Board • Books, travel, entertainment and all other	• Faculty and staff salaries • Operation and maintenance of plant • Supplies and equipment • Amortization and depreciation of plant
Parents	Any parental contribution toward children's educational living expenses	Tuition fees as paid by parents, net of any portion covered by grants, scholarships or loan subsidies
Students	Any student contribution from savings or own assets . . . plus term-time work, and summer savings . . . plus loans net of governmental subsidies	Tuition fees as paid by students, net of any portion covered by grants, scholarships or loan subsidies
Taxpayers	Any student grants, need-based or otherwise, for costs of living . . . plus any direct governmental subsidies specifically for students' room and board . . . plus indirect subsidies via tax preferences to parents of students or repayment subsidies	Educational and general portions of public institution budgets, net of any revenues derived directly from students or parents via tuition fees . . . plus any portion of tuition fee revenue that is covered by governmental grants or loan subsidies . . . plus governmental grants to private institutions
Institutions/Philanthropists	Scholarships or grants to defray living costs supported by endowment earnings or current gifts	Current gifts or endowment earnings for the support of basic instructional budgets plus any portion of philanthropically originated scholarships covering tuition fees
Business* (consumers, employees, or shareholders)	Scholarships or grants to defray livings costs through gifts to institutions	Unrestricted gifts to institutions plus any portion of tuition fees paid on behalf of employees or other grant recipients

* Business is presented here as a potential fifth source of revenue. The true incidence, or impact, of business contributions, however, is passed on to consumers, employees, shareholders or even to the general taxpayer. For this reason, as explained in the text, and because its contributions are generally minor, 'business' will not be covered in this text as an independent fifth 'bearer of costs'.

fund, the burden of that contribution actually falls on some combination of the following:

- the consumers of the product or service produced by that business, as the cost of the contribution, like all production costs, is passed on to be reflected in the price;
- the general taxpayer, who must make up the revenue lost from the tax deduction that lowers taxes and lessens the burden that would otherwise be felt in the business;
- the employee, whose compensation package may include a tuition fee grant programme, but only inasmuch as some other element of compensation, including a possibility of additional cash wage, is forgone;
- the shareholder or owner, whose profits may decline as a result of contributions made to higher education, but only to the extent that the costs incurred are not absorbed or mitigated by the consumer, general taxpayer or employee as suggested above.

Industry or business is not an ultimate bearer of costs in the manner of students, parents, taxpayers and donors, but is rather an intermediary that in turn passes the costs on to consumers, employees, general taxpayers or shareholders. Business remains a potentially significant player in that it can support higher education to an extent that the ultimate bearers of this burden – i.e. the consumers – might not voluntarily choose to do. In this sense, the business contribution may be likened most to the taxpayer contribution, particularly within a typically European consumption-based tax system. But because of the difficulty in specifying the true ultimate incidence of the business contribution, and because such contributions are still relatively small even in the United States and even less significant elsewhere, this study will not further consider business as a separate contributor, or bearer of cost, and will instead deal with the three principal participants of parent, student and taxpayer.

Cost sharing in the United Kingdom, the Federal Republic of Germany, France, Sweden and the United States
Four European countries were chosen to provide a basis for comparison with the United States, and a comparative analysis of cost sharing:

- the United Kingdom, because of the extensive literature available and the extremely generous grants combined with a virtual zero 'self-help' (i.e. student-borne) expectation;

- the Federal Republic of Germany, because of its highly developed needs-analysis system and its recent changeover from a mostly grant to an all-loan (albeit very highly subsidized) system;
- France, because of a national needs-analysis system quite different from that employed in the United States, a very strong tradition of parental support, and a substantial literature on the economics of higher education; and
- Sweden, because it has been a leader in the world in the use of student loans and has also moved away completely from any expected parental contributions.

The four European nations were visited during the summer of 1985. From this information, profiles were developed on higher education generally, and cost sharing specifically, for each of the four European countries and the United States. Special attention was paid to securing comparable data on:

- the total out-of-pocket costs of higher education as faced by students and their parents;
- the expected parental contribution, if any, and how it is derived from income and other factors;
- the expected student contribution, from savings, term-time work, and/or loans;
- the taxpayer-borne contribution, whether from need-based grants, loan subsidies or indirect support of student living expenses;
- the institutional/philanthropic contribution (in the United States);
- trends and issues regarding the sharing of higher education costs within each country; and
- problems or issues common to all five countries.

Summary observations on sharing and shifting the costs of higher education

The five systems studied are very different and yet very alike. They are quite different (more so than had been anticipated) in the basic costs faced by the student and the family. They differ greatly in their approaches to what Americans would call 'financial aid', and the resulting shares borne by parents, students and taxpayers differ considerably for students and families from similar circumstances. But the countries are substantially alike in their dependence for meeting these costs upon parents (except for Sweden), students (except for the United Kingdom), taxpayers and institutions/philanthropists (mainly

the United States). They are also alike in that they all profess to bring
higher education into the reach of all who are qualified, without regard
to family socio-economic status. And most employ concepts and tools
familiar to the field of student finance: need analyses, expected
parental contributions, governmentally sponsored student loans, and
the like. This chapter summarizes and analyses these similarities and
differences, attempting as much as possible to control for differences
in family income, and expressing the costs of higher education and the
value of student support in terms of constant purchasing power parity
rates. The chapter summarizes the position in 1985-86, i.e. before
some of the changes described later in this book.

The costs to the student and family
The great difference between the United States and most of Europe
with regard to costs and student financial assistance is that the students
in the United Kingdom, France, the Federal Republic of Germany and
Sweden pay almost no part of the costs of instruction – that is, pay zero
or minuscule tuition fees – whereas US students pay a small but
noticeable portion of these costs in the public sector and a very large
portion in the private, or independent, sector. Because the principal
interest of this study was in the policies and policy instruments that fall
within the concept of 'financial assistance', the unit of observation was
those costs faced by the student and his or her family.

In the United Kingdom, the Federal Republic of Germany, France
and Sweden, this meant only the costs of student living (except for
some *Grandes Ecoles* students in France who pay tuition fees). In the
United States, the costs faced by the student and family include, of
course, the costs of student living plus tuition fees.

Figure 2.1 shows a variety of cost estimates for each of the five
countries in the study. There is considerable variation both within each
country and among the five countries. Within-country variation can be
attributed to commuter–resident status (i.e. whether students live at
home or in college), to the amount of tuition fees paid (in the United
States and to a limited degree in France), and to individual student
living standards, which in turn are probably very largely a function of
resources available to the student–family unit. Between-country
variation can be attributed to the presence or absence of tuition fees,
to the general cost of living, to the extent of governmentally subsidized
room and board, and to the prevailing cultural sense of how well a
student ought to live – in comparison, say, with his or her non-student
age peers.

For example, discounting tuition fees, the costs among the five countries studied are highest in Sweden, reflecting the general high cost of living in that country, the absence of governmental subsidization of living expenses, and a cultural view that expects a 21-year-old student to live at about the same standard as a 21-year-old employee. The costs in Germany are also quite high and would be higher were it not for some savings made possible by the governmentally subsidized *Studentenwerke,* which provide low-cost meals and some low-cost housing. French costs are the lowest, due to lower livings costs generally (compared to Sweden, the United States or Germany); to the subsidized meals and housing available from the local *Centre Regional des Oeuvres Universitaires et Scolaires,* or CROUS; and finally to a tradition in which living either at home or in genteel academic poverty continues to be a more accepted condition of student life than, say, in the United Kingdom, the Federal Republic of Germany or Scandinavia. The United Kingdom estimates are low partly because of its lower living standards in general and possibly because the only estimates available were either from the Department of Education and Science, which may have some incentive to estimate low in order to restrain the growth of grant expenditures, or actual survey results from the National Union of Students, which may also err on the low side as expenditure surveys often do. However, taking all factors into consideration, including inevitable errors in estimation and controlling, especially for commuter-resident status in each country, and for tuition fees in the United States, the costs faced by students and families in the five countries portrayed in Figure 2.1 are quite similar.

The parental contribution
Comparative expected parental contributions are shown in Figure 2.2 as a function of income and also in Figures 2.3, 2.4 and 2.5 as a proportion of total revenues for different parental income assumptions. Among the five countries studied, only in Sweden (but also elsewhere in Scandinavia) are parents not officially expected to contribute towards the direct living expenses of their children in higher education. Some contributions are still common from middle- and higher-income parents, either to provide their children with higher student living standards or to lessen some of their children's dependence on loans, but the direct burden of higher education costs on parents in Sweden is the lightest at all income levels.

In fairness to Swedish parents, who may not feel their burdens so light, carrying as they do the greatest overall tax burden of the five

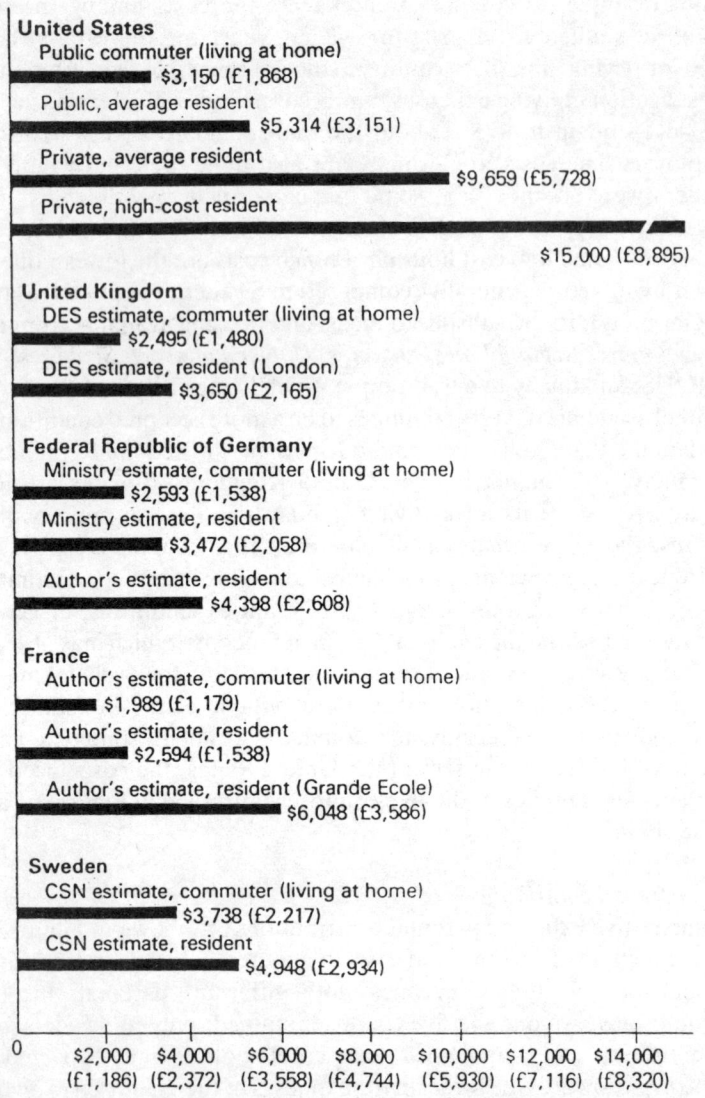

United States
  Public commuter (living at home)
    $3,150 (£1,868)
  Public, average resident
    $5,314 (£3,151)
  Private, average resident
    $9,659 (£5,728)
  Private, high-cost resident
    $15,000 (£8,895)

United Kingdom
  DES estimate, commuter (living at home)
    $2,495 (£1,480)
  DES estimate, resident (London)
    $3,650 (£2,165)

Federal Republic of Germany
  Ministry estimate, commuter (living at home)
    $2,593 (£1,538)
  Ministry estimate, resident
    $3,472 (£2,058)
  Author's estimate, resident
    $4,398 (£2,608)

France
  Author's estimate, commuter (living at home)
    $1,989 (£1,179)
  Author's estimate, resident
    $2,594 (£1,538)
  Author's estimate, resident (Grande Ecole)
    $6,048 (£3,586)

Sweden
  CSN estimate, commuter (living at home)
    $3,738 (£2,217)
  CSN estimate, resident
    $4,948 (£2,934)

| 0 | $2,000 (£1,186) | $4,000 (£2,372) | $6,000 (£3,558) | $8,000 (£4,744) | $10,000 (£5,930) | $12,000 (£7,116) | $14,000 (£8,320) |

Figure 2.1. Costs faced by students and their families, United States, United Kingdom, Federal Republic of Germany, France and Sweden, various estimates, 1985-86

Note: The figures in brackets show the costs expressed in £ sterling, using the 1985 purchasing power parity rate of $1 = £0.593.

countries studied, the cost of higher education weighs on all parents as taxpayers as well as upon those parents who have themselves attended the university, many of whom will be paying off their own study means loans for many years – not unlike paying an annual surtax for the privilege of having attended the university. Also in fairness to Sweden's social welfare system, the nation has achieved such a level of equality in the distribution of income that it is not considered necessary or even appropriate to charge the system of financing higher education with the additional task of further redistributing the nation's income. With these caveats, however, the Swedish parents *qua* parents, particularly those with higher incomes and with several university-bound children, clearly benefit *vis-à-vis* parents in the other countries in this study, with the student especially and also those taxpayers without children in college carrying a commensurately heavier burden.

Figure 2.2. Higher education expenses borne by parents as a function of family income, United Kingdom, Federal Republic of Germany, France, Sweden and the United States, 1985-86.

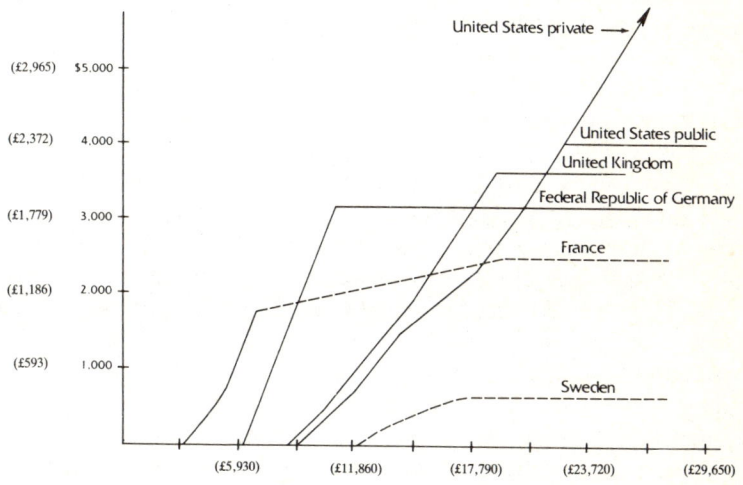

Note: The figures in brackets show the approximate purchasing power parity rate in 1985 ($1 = £0.593).

The greatest burden on the low-income parents seems to be in France, where Figure 2.2 shows the need-based grant reduction (and hence the implicit expectation of a parental contribution) beginning at a very low income. The cash costs of university attendance in France tend to be low, but the proportion of those costs borne by parents among low-income families, as shown in Figure 2.3, is quite high.

The Federal Republic of Germany also begins its expected parental contributions at a rather low annual income, at least in comparison to the United Kingdom and the United States (and of course to Sweden, with its absence of any expected parental contribution). Both the French and German expected parental contributions rise in a very steep functional relationship to annual income, constituting in effect a very high marginal tax rate on income beginning with the modest income at which a contribution is first expected (and the *bourse* or *BAföG* begins to be reduced) and continuing as incomes rise until that income at which the *bourse* and *BAföG* are phased out altogether and parental contributions have presumably taken their places. Such a severe means testing supports the general French and West German proposition that the expenses of student maintenance are fundamentally and properly *family* expenses (shared, perhaps, by both parents and students) and that the principal taxpayer responsibility is only for a sharply targeted programme of assistance to the very poor.

The UK and the US public-college expected parental contributions are very similar, as shown in Figure 2.2. Both begin at higher income levels than in either France or Germany, thus placing less burden on low- and lower-middle-income families, and both rise in less steeply sloped relationships to income, reaching maximum parental contributions (and phasing out the taxpayer-borne contributions) at parental incomes in the $30,000-$40,000 (£18,000-£24,000) range. For the United Kingdom, this means that the great majority of families are eligible for grants and that a substantial number, even from the lower middle-income families, need make no contributions at all to the higher educational costs of their children. In contrast to the French and West German systems, which leave student living expenses to the parents and students except when incomes are very low, the UK system leaves at least the bulk of them to taxpayers (i.e. governmental grants) except when parental incomes are high.

The parental contribution in the United States is very light at low and lower-middle incomes but becomes very substantial at upper-middle and higher incomes, as shown in Figures 2.3, 2.4 and 2.5, for families with children attending private colleges because of the need to pass on tuition costs, to both parents and students. Part of this heavy parental burden reflects the higher cost of instruction at US colleges, most of which have much more extensive physical plants, non-academic student support services and administrative support than do their European counterparts. In addition, however, the heavy parental burden at upper-middle and higher incomes reflects a public policy decision in the United States (albeit more historically derived than consciously decided upon) to allow much of higher education to be both operated and financed privately, thus implicitly relieving the public sector and the taxpayer of what would otherwise have been their burdens, and instead to pass on more of these actual instructional costs to students and parents as the presumed prime recipients and beneficiaries. While the low-income parents in the United States continue to be relieved of this burden even when their children are attending the high-cost private colleges, thus reflecting the use of need-based grants in the United States as a general economic welfare tool, the upper-middle- and high-income parents of college-going children, enjoying a lighter overall tax burden than their West European counterparts, pay a 'user charge' via college tuition fees that are extremely high for those electing to send children to private colleges and by comparison even for those whose children attend the public colleges and universities. This perspective contrasts most sharply with the Swedish viewpoint, which assumes the costs of higher education to be the joint responsibility of the student and the general taxpayer and which rejects not only the concept of parental responsibility but also the use of need-based, or means-tested, grants as a tool of general social welfare or income redistribution.

The student contribution
Student contributions are shown in Figures 2.3, 2.4, and 2.5 for students for low-, middle- and high-income families. The students' share of costs is highest in the United States for low- and middle-income students attending higher-cost private colleges, but it is most consistently high, particularly as a share of total needed revenues, in Sweden. It is relatively high in the Federal Republic of Germany, although the high initial debt burden of German youth from low- and lower-middle-income families is greatly reduced by the extent of repayment subsidies within the loan system. In all three countries, governmentally sponsored programmes make student loans available at subsidized rates, with long repayment periods and without any tests of credit worthiness *per se*. The United States is the only country among the five studied that encourages part-time student employment to the extent of subsidizing colleges, universities and other public agencies for hiring students.

The students' share of higher education costs is relatively low in France, which lacks a generally available, governmentally sponsored

Figure 2.3. Sharing the costs of higher education for low-income families in the United Kingdom, Federal Republic of Germany, France, Sweden and the United States, 1985-86.

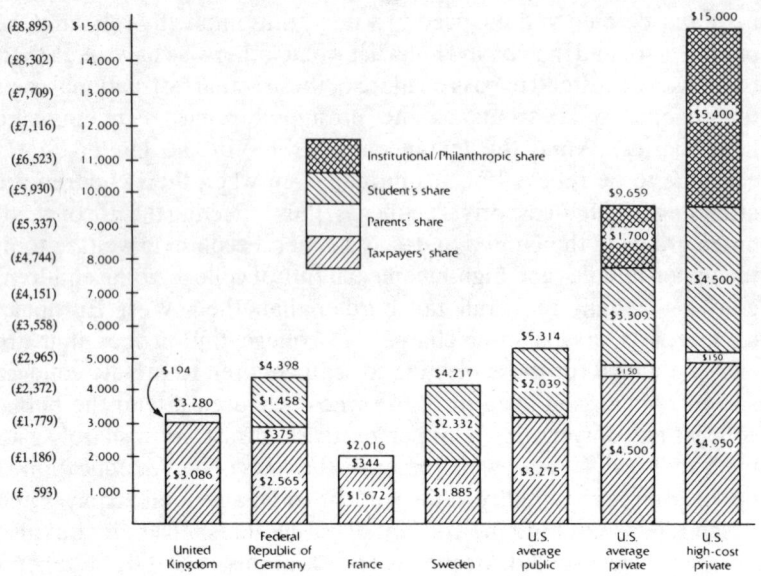

Note: The figures in brackets show the approximate purchasing power parity rate in 1985 ($1 = £0.593).

loan programme, although students who are not *bourse* recipients (thus excluding those from the poorest families) are allowed and even encouraged to take part-time jobs and there are many small, unsubsidized loan programmes available at least to special (e.g. *Grandes Ecoles*) students.

The students' share is by far the lowest among these five nations in the United Kingdom, which not only has no governmentally sponsored loans programmes (and the students and the opposition clearly intend to keep it that way), but also actively discourages students from working part time.

Although this study did not examine extensive trend data, it has shown that the students' share of expenses has been increasing over the past decade or so in the United States and in Sweden, and it can certainly be said to have increased in the Federal Republic of Germany with the 1984 conversion of the *BAföG* from a mainly grant to an

Figure 2.4. Sharing the costs of higher education for middle-income families in the United Kingdom, Federal Republic of Germany, France, Sweden and the United States, 1985-86.

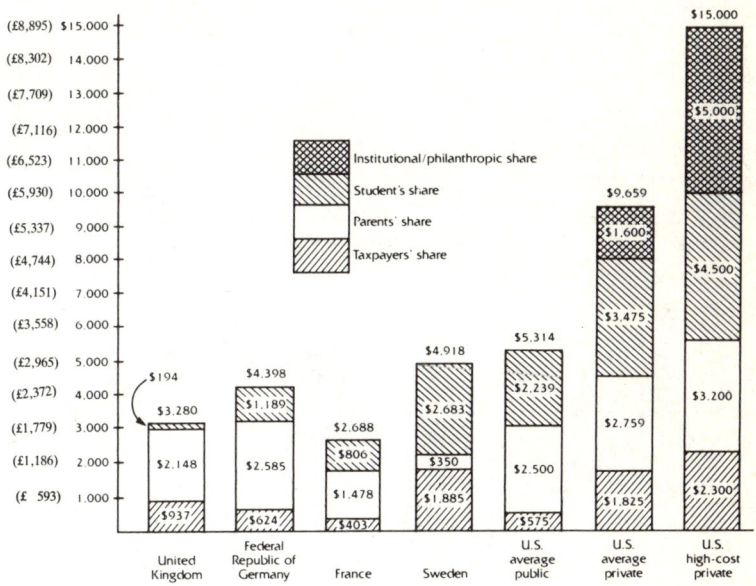

Note: The figures in brackets show the approximate purchasing power parity rate in 1985 ($1 = £0.593).

all-loan programme. This trend is of concern in part because of the possible problems in connection with rising student debts, e.g. rising defaults, declining respect for obligations or the alleged distortion of career choices. Of equal concern is the shift of costs from parents and taxpayers on to students, seemingly without public awareness and thus perhaps with neither rationale nor intent.

Student loans and choice
The rationale for a student loan programme follows the rationale for the student bearing a portion of the cost of higher education: Whatever that portion is to be, there must be generally available loans so that students with no current income or assets of their own can meet their share of expenses and repay when they are finished at college, are earning a living and presumably are reaping some of the monetary

Figure 2.5. Sharing the costs of higher education for high-income families in the United Kingdom, Federal Republic of Germany, France, Sweden and the United States, 1985-86.

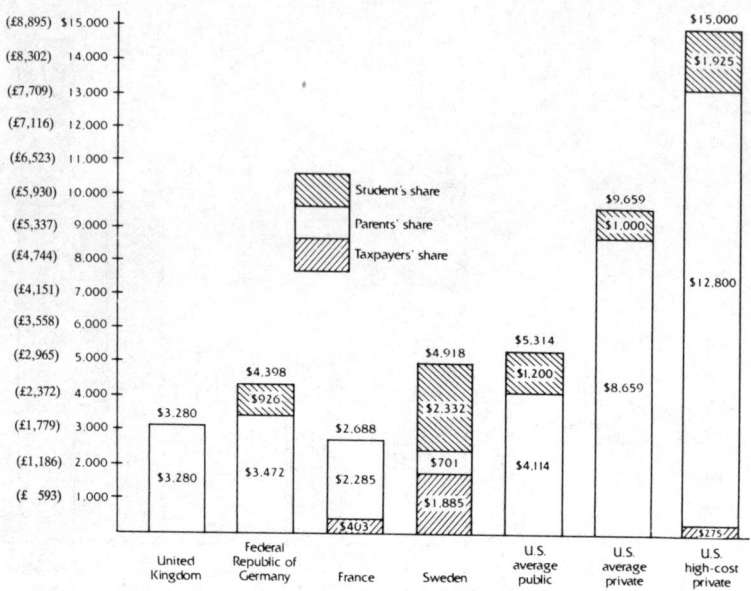

Note: The figures in brackets show the approximate purchasing power parity rate in 1985 ($1 = £0.593).

benefits of their higher education. Because most students have neither established credit nor collateral, it is essential that a policy requiring the student to pay a portion of the costs be supported either by governmental guarantees, as in the US Guaranteed Student Loans, or by direct provision of governmental capital, as in the Swedish study means, German *BAföG* or US National Direct Student Loans.

There are no generally available, non-governmentally sponsored student loans in any country. Hence, where there is no such governmentally sponsored loan programme – as in the United Kingdom or in France – it is very difficult to sustain a policy that assumes any substantial portion of costs being borne by the student. This, of course, is the cornerstone of the students' position in the United Kingdom that no student loan programme of any type whatsoever should be established: once in place, it is feared that it would be all too easy to shift costs from the taxpayer or parent or both to the student. With no available loans whatsoever, the government remains under great pressure to maintain its grants, to the obvious benefit of the students.

However, student loans also serve, on a much smaller basis, a function quite apart from support of an overall policy of student cost-sharing. This is the provision of choice to students who, for whatever reason, are excluded by public policy from the taxpayer grants that would have been available or who for some reason are denied the otherwise expected contribtution from their parents – but who, were loans to be available, would be willing to borrow in order to supplant the missing taxpayer or parental contribution and to invest in their own higher education. Were student loans available in the United Kingdom, for example, students denied the mandatory grant or the parental contribution offset would at least have a chance to proceed on their own – with no change in the fundamental, underlying policy of no student share for the regular student. Similarly, the French student who had been denied help from his or her parents, or who wished to live away from home, would also be able to do so with the assistance of a generally available student loan programme, again with no diminution of the current commitment to taxpayer-borne assistance, which is very minimal anyway.

A similar observation may be made where student loans are available, but at such enormous subsidy and cost to the taxpayer that they must be rationed according to some standard of need. For example, what of the German student who is denied a *BAföG* loan because of his or her parents' income, but who very much needs to borrow to enable a certain living standard or to make up for a shortfall in the parental contribution (in lieu of taking them to family court)? Or what of the Swedish student needing or wanting to borrow a bit more than the maximum study means in order to make up for what is generally believed to have been an erosion over time of the real purchasing power of that assistance? Were student loans to be generally available at a rate of interest not far below the true cost of money, such borrowing could easily take place with no more justification than the understandably high present value placed on money by students with no alternative means of receiving a higher education. However, the strict need-based rationing of these loans, made necessary by their very high subsidies, precludes them from being easily used either to fill in for shortfalls in the parental contribution or simply to provide a somewhat-higher-than-minimal standard of student living. Such loans of choice or convenience are unavailable altogether in the United Kingdom or France and are virtually unavailable in Sweden and West Germany. Only in the United States, and only with the supplement of the relatively high-cost, market-rate Auxiliary Loans to Assist Students (ALAS), now called Supplementary Loans for Students, are students able to borrow as much as they reasonably need purely as an expression of their time preference for money and their faith in sufficient private returns to their investments in education.

Sharing the costs: who should pay?

The proper apportioning of costs is a matter of intense public policy debate in the United States and Western Europe. Specifically, what is the relative share of costs to be borne by parents, students and the general taxpayer?

The aim of a comparative study is to deepen and broaden our understanding of why countries have developed their particular responses to their similar challenges, how and why one's own country has developed as it has, and what it might take to change a given system in a particular way. The fundamental question of who should pay has been faced in all the countries of this study. Answers have been provided from the perspectives of economic theory, political ideology and culture, but none of these perspectives provides the whole answer.

The proper apportioning of costs between parents, students and taxpayers is not easily arrived at through a traditional division of benefits thought to be 'public' or 'private'. Nor is a country's generosity with taxpayer-borne grants – or, conversely, its readiness to pass the burden on to students through loans – predictable merely from the general socio-economic ideology of the party in political power. Rather, the sharing of the costs at any one time and the underlying policies and programmes of need-based grants, expected parental contributions, student loans programmes and the like are linked to such social, political and economic factors as: the balance of national concern for equality versus meritocratic rewards, the prevailing wage differentials between the graduates of the secondary and tertiary educational levels, the political power of students, the general economic climate and in particular the status of the public treasury, etc. In fact, what is probably more interesting and useful is not one or another particular apportioning of these costs at a point in time, but rather the probable consequences of proposed changes or shifts in one or another share, to which this concluding section now turns.

Shifting the costs: the dynamics of cost sharing

The initial premise of this study was that the costs of higher education have to be met by three principal sources: parents, students and taxpayers, with institutions or philanthropists a fourth source of some significance at least in the United States. A basic corollary to this premise is that a change in the share borne by one party must either mean a change in the shares of one or both of the others, or else a change in something even more fundamental, such as the living standards of students or the socio-economic profile of the student body. For example a significant decline over time in taxpayer-borne, need-based grants must mean either a corresponding decline in the standard of student living, a decline in the proportion of students judged to be needy, an increase in the contributions of at least some parents, or an increase in the contributions of at least some students – or some combination of the above.

The most important benefit from a comparative study such as this may be the greater understanding that can emerge from an array of examples of the intended and unintended consequences of changes in one or another of the policy tools of higher educational finance. For example:

1. Decreasing the average size of need-based grants (as in the United States since 1980)

   - may, but probably will not, because of the income levels involved, lead to increased parental contributions;
   - may lead some students to reduce their overall expenses by choosing a lower-cost (priced) public college rather than a higher-cost (priced) private one; and
   - may lead to higher annual and aggregate student debts.

2. Increasing taxpayer-borne grants to needy students (as is proposed by students in most countries in most years)

   - maintains the standard of student living, assuming the increase to be commensurate with the rising costs of student life;
   - gives the student options (e.g. to attend a higher-cost institution or one farther from home); and
   - may lessen the need to borrow or to work part time or both.

3. Introducing a programme of taxpayer-borne grants, or tax credits, to students and/or families on bases other than financial need (as at one time proposed by the Reagan Administration in the United States)

- allows the student to increase his or her standard of living;
- allows the student to borrow less or work fewer part-time hours; or
- allows the parents to reduce their contributions accordingly, in which case neither of the other two possibilities will happen and parents of bright young people will become the prime beneficiaries.

4. Reducing taxpayer-borne grant benefits dollar-for-dollar for student earnings (as in France)

   - will discourage part-time work and thus reduce student living standards, but only for the very lowest-income students who have a chance of a grant anyway.

5. Opening up the availability of highly subsidized student loans without regard to need (as in the United States in 1978)

   - encourages all students to borrow to the maximum allowed, with much of the resulting borrowing either displacing what would otherwise have been the parental contribution or allowing the student to reinvest the borrowed funds at a higher rate of interest.

6. Maintaining very low interest rates and high subsidies within the student loan programme (as in the Federal Republic of Germany and Sweden, especially)

   - increases the taxpayer-borne share of costs; and
   - incurs the phenomenon listed immediately above; or
   - requires all loans to be rationed strictly according to need, which in turn precludes a student from choosing to borrow in lieu of a parental contribution.

7. Making student loans generally available where they now are not (as might be done in United Kingdom or France)

   - may begin a steady erosion of taxpayer-borne grants and parental contributions as both other sources see relief from their burdens in the expansion of student loans; and
   - would give at least the choice of higher education, at some personal costs, to students otherwise ineligible for grants or unsupported by their parents.

8. Introducing tuition fees where there currently are none (as might be

the case in France, the Federal Republic of Germany or Sweden)

- in Sweden, would increase student debts even more, as well as the taxpayer-borne subsidies thereof;
- in Germany, could lead to the costs of tuition being shared in almost any desired proportion: *BAföG* recipients, through higher debts; parents of *BAföG* recipients, through higher parental contribution; non-*BAföG* recipients and their parents, in whatever way expenses are now shared, presumably mainly by parents; and taxpayers, through *BAföG* subsidies; and
- in France, would increase mainly the parental-borne costs, which would place considerable hardship on low-income families, for whom the *bourse* is now barely adequate.

9. Covering tuition fees with taxpayer-borne grants only in case of need, i.e. making the tuition grant means tested (as was proposed in the United Kingdom in late 1984)

- would increase costs paid by the highest-income parents; and
- would reduce slightly the taxpayer-borne burden, or else allow the increased net tuition revenues to be retained and spent by the institutions.

There are few right or wrong policies in the comparative study of almost any field. To most Americans, the UK system looks a bit odd because of the absence of a student contribution; the Swedish system because of no parental contribution; the French because of such a seemingly meagre taxpayer-borne contribution and all the disincentives to studying away from home; and the German system because of the political blood that was shed over a student-loan programme so heavily subsidized that the true costs are still borne overwhelmingly by the taxpayer. The US system, if it may be called that, must in turn look odd to colleagues from these other countries because of the aggressive competition on the part of institutions for students; the coexistence of public, private non-profit making and proprietary profit-making institutions of post-secondary and higher education; the high tuition fees paid in the private sector and yet the competitive robustness of most of that sector *vis-à-vis* the lower-priced public sector; the bewildering array of grant and loan programmes; and the almost total individualization of the ultimate price to the student and his or her family. In its own way, though, each national system is trying to assure equality of opportunity; to provide necessary funding for the universities; to become no more, and perhaps even a bit less, of a burden to the taxpayers; and to avoid undue political antagonisms on the part of either parents or students.

Reference

Johnstone, D. B. (1986), *Sharing the Costs of Higher Education: student financial assistance in the United Kingdom, the Federal Republic of Germany, France, Sweden and the United States.* New York: College Entrance Examination Board.

Chapter Three
Cost-Sharing in Higher Education: The United States Experience
Janet S. Hansen

Bruce Johnstone has observed that, 'compared probably to all other nations in the world, US colleges and universities rely on more diverse sources of revenue and especially on more non-governmental (or non-taxpayer) sources' (Johnstone, 1986). Indeed, the major financing partners he identifies – taxpayers, parents, students and institutions/philanthropists – share the burdens of paying for college more equally than in many countries. American taxpayers bear relatively less responsibility for the direct support of institutions, all of which charge some student fees and some of which are privately rather than publicly sponsored. Parents and students bear the primary responsibility for meeting tuition charges and living expenses, although institutions and state and federal taxpayers have gradually assumed a portion of this responsibility as well through the programmes we call student financial assistance.

This chapter explores how the United States shares the burden of student support – that is, paying for tuition and living expenses – and the issues we are currently addressing that have relevance for other countries. At the conclusion, I shall try to draw out some specific lessons from our American experience with student financial aid that speak to questions being asked about student support systems in the United Kingdom and elsewhere.

The evolution of a financing partnership
Before the mid-1960s, the burden of paying college expenses fell almost entirely on parents and students. What financial assistance was available came mostly from colleges themselves. A few states had grant and/or loan programmes, and the federal government had put a toe into the water when it created loans for financially needy students as

part of the post-Sputnik National Defense Education Act in 1958.[1] There had been talk of expanding federal aid to students since the post-World War II GI Bill for veterans successfully brought thousands of students into post-secondary education, but political conditions in the 1950s did not favour an increasing role for the federal government in higher education finance. Specially-targeted federal aid to veterans continued after the Korean War, but proposals for more general student assistance languished.

This situation changed dramatically in 1964 and 1965. As part of the broad assault on social problems of the 'War on Poverty,' Congress and President Lyndon Johnson approved a College Work-Study programme in 1964 to subsidize employment for financially needy college students and an Educational Opportunity Grant Program for such students in 1965. (The latter is now called Supplemental Educational Opportunity Grants.) In addition, the Guaranteed Student Loan Program was enacted in 1965 aimed primarily at middle-income students whose families, while not financially needy, might want help with cash flow demands during the college years. Along with the previously enacted National Defense Student Loans Program for needy students, a triad of federal programmes (grant, loan, work) was now in place that paralleled the student aid structure created in earlier years by colleges themselves. In addition, Congress modified the social security programme to allow children of deceased or disabled workers to receive educational benefits if they were enrolled in higher education, rather than ending social security support at the age of 18.

In the next few years pressures grew not only to enlarge the available aid but to make it more predictable. Students went directly to banks to obtain Guaranteed Student Loans (GSLs), but the other federal aid was awarded by colleges and universities from federal appropriations. Thus students could not know the amount of their aid, or whether they would even be eligible for assistance, until they applied to college and had been accepted. This process seemed at odds with the educational opportunity goals of the programmes. In 1972, therefore, the federal government created the Basic Educational Opportunity Grant Program (now called Pell Grants). These grants were meant to provide a reliable financial foundation upon which each student might add other student assistance from various sources and contributions from parents and from his or her own efforts. Students would apply for the new grants directly to the federal government, and grant amounts would for the most part be independent of where the student ultimately enrolled. In addition to Pell Grants, the federal government in 1972 created State Student Incentive Grants (SSIGs) to encourage all states to enact or expand their own grant programmes. The older programmes were left in place; student aid supporters were unwilling to count on generous funding for Pell grants. As it happened, though, the Pell programme grew quickly.

Even as these grants were phased in, however, new pressures were building. Interest in tuition tax credits for middle-income families, a subject that comes and goes on the American political landscape, made a reappearance. Middle-income families – those who don't feel rich and who don't qualify for need-based student aid – clamoured for help with college expenses. To deflect interest in tax credits, President Jimmy Carter and Congress approved the Middle Income Student Assistance Act in 1978. Pell Grant eligibility was expanded up the income scale; and all students, regardless of income, were made eligible for Guaranteed Student Loans (GSLs).

A combination of factors led to an almost immediate backlash against the changes enacted in 1978. Unexpectedly high inflation made GSLs, with their fixed 7 per cent interest rate, exceedingly attractive college financing vehicles; and loan volume exploded. Federal costs associated with loan subsidies exploded as well. Then, in 1980 Ronald Reagan was elected to the presidency, pledging to curtail federal spending on all social programmes and questioning the role of the federal government in supporting college students.

Throughout its years in office, the Reagan Administration tried to scale back federal student assistance. Most of its proposals were soundly defeated by Congress, except for the phase-out of social security student benefits. Nevertheless, the rapid growth in federal aid that characterized the 1970s came to a halt. The purchasing power of federal student assistance actually declined for several years and is still below 1980-81 levels. States and institutions picked up the pace of their spending but were unable to compensate fully for the federal losses. The eligibility changes made in 1978 were repealed, and legislation enacted at various points during the 1980s restricted GSLs to students who can qualify on the basis of a financial need test.

The only new programme initiatives came in the loan area. Parent Loans for Undergraduate Students (PLUS), a less-subsidized version of GSL, enabled parents to borrow regardless of income with minimal federal subsidy. Supplemental Loans for Students (SLS) expanded access to loans for certain kinds of students (graduate students and undergraduates not financially dependent on their parents), again at minimal subsidy. Income Contingent Loans (ICL) involved a very small-scale demonstration project experimenting with new kinds of repayment schedules in the Perkins Loan programme, the 1958 loan plan whose name has been changed several times. Another name change was enacted in 1988, when Congress changed the name of Guaranteed Student Loan to Stafford Loans, in honour of retiring Senator Robert T Stafford. These are still generally known as Guaranteed Student Loans (GSLs), however, and this name is used in this chapter.

The current pattern of student assistance in the United States is not the result of a grand design but has evolved over the years to meet problems and perceived shortcomings. This evolution is captured in statistical terms in Tables 3.1 and 3.2, which show aid awarded in selected years to students in post-secondary education from all federal sources and from state and institutional grants in current dollars (Table 3.1) and in dollars adjusted for inflation (Table 3.2).[2]

Even though taxpayer support has grown dramatically over the past three decades, the other partners in higher education finance still bear a large responsibility for meeting college costs. A survey of undergraduates enrolled in the autumn of 1986 indicates that only 45 per cent received student aid from any source, with about 35 per cent reporting some federal assistance. Only 38 per cent of all undergraduates received grant assistance; the remaining aid recipients received help in the form of loans and/or subsidized work opportunities. This leaves a large share of higher education expenses for parents and students to pay. Moreover, while families express increasing concern about their ability to pay college costs (more on this later), there continues to be widespread support for the idea that these expenses should be shared among a variety of partners and that parents and students should, along with taxpayers and institutions/ philanthropists, bear a significant part of the responsibility of paying for higher education.

The shifting burden of paying for college
While burden-sharing remains a widely-accepted basis for American college financing, the specific responsibilities of each partner are subject to dispute. As the preceding section suggests, the relative roles of each partner have shifted over time. Sometimes these shifts have resulted from explicit policy decisions. Especially in recent years, the shifts have occurred more as a result of general economic and fiscal pressures rather than a strong desire on the part of policy makers to

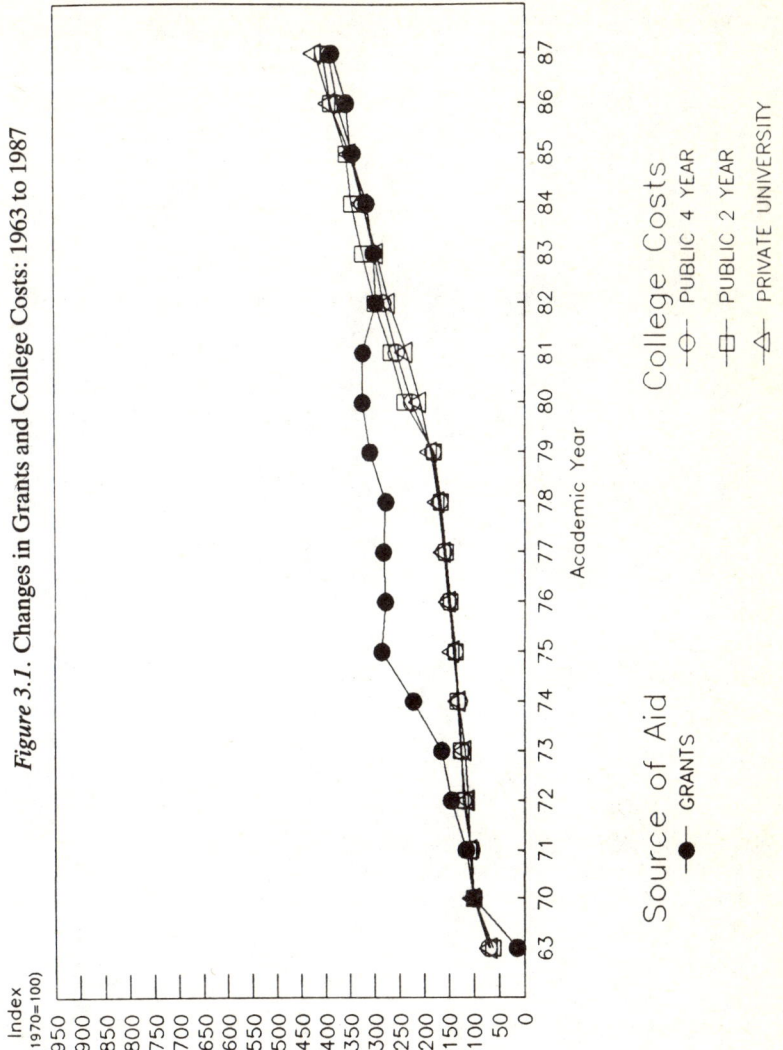

Figure 3.1. Changes in Grants and College Costs: 1963 to 1987

Table 3.1. Aid Awarded to Post-secondary Students in Current 1987 Dollars (Millions)

			Academic Year			Estimated
Federally supported programmes	1963-64	1970-71	1975-76	1980-81	1985-86	1987-88
Generally available aid						
Pell	0	0	937	2,387	3,567	3,739
SEOG	0	134	201	368	410	396
SSIG	0	0	20	77	76	76
CWS	0	227	295	660	656	665
Perkins (NDSL)	114	241	460	694	703	853
ICL						5
GSL, PLUS and SLS	0	1,015	1,267	6,203	8,839	11,270
(GSL)				(6,200)	(8,328)	(8,976)
(SLS)					(265)	(1,776)
(PLUS)				(3)	(246)	(517)
Subtotal	114	1,617	3,179	10,388	14,251	17,002
Specially directed aid						
Social security	0	499	1,093	1,883	0	0
Veterans	67	1,121	4,180	1,714	849	773
Military			39	203	346	359
Other grants	9	16	63	121	68	72
Other loans	0	42	45	62	372	234
Subtotal	76	1,678	5,420	3,988	1,635	1,440
Total federal aid	190	3,295	8,639	14,376	15,887	18,442
State grant programmes	56	236	490	801	1,311	1,540
Institutionally awarded aid	300	965	1,435	2,060	3,674	4,565
Total federal, state and institutional aid	546	4,496	4,219	17,237	20,871	24,547

Table 3.2. Aid Awarded to Post-secondary Students in Constant 1987 Dollars (Millions)

	Academic Year					
Federally supported programmes	1963-64	1970-71	1975-76	1980-81	1985-86	1987-88
Generally available aid						
Pell	0	0	1,918	3,132	3,725	3,669
SEOG	0	382	412	483	428	389
SSIG	0	0	40	101	79	74
CWS	0	650	604	866	685	652
Perkins (NDSL)	418	688	942	910	734	837
ICL						5
GSL, PLUS and SLS	0	2,903	2,595	8,140	9,229	11,059
(GSL)				(8,136)	(8,696)	(8,809)
(SLS)					(277)	(1,743)
(PLUS)				(3)	(257)	(508)
Subtotal	418	4,624	6,511	13,632	14,881	16,685
Specially directed aid						
Social security	0	1,427	2,239	2,471	0	0
Veterans	248	3,208	8,561	2,250	887	759
Military			68	267	361	353
Other grants	32	45	129	159	71	71
Other loans	0	120	92	82	389	230
Subtotal	280	4,800	11,089	5,128	1,527	1,242
Total federal aid	689	9,425	17,600	18,865	16,588	18,098
State grant programmes	206	675	1,004	1,051	1,369	1,512
Institutionally awarded aid	1,104	2,760	2,939	2,703	3,836	4,480
Total federal, state and institutional aid	2,009	12,860	21,543	22,619	21,793	24,809

alter the balance of responsibility for meeting college costs.

Data about who pays how much for higher education in the large and diverse American system are frustratingly elusive. Only in 1986-87 did the federal government begin a triennial survey on financing patterns, so it will be many years before we can observe trends. In the meantime, we can find evidence of shifting burdens in existing statistics.

One indication comes from looking at how grant and loan availability has changed over time in relationship to college costs. In Figures 3.1 and 3.2 college costs in representative sectors of American higher education have been indexed along with grant aid (Figure 3.1) and loans (Figure 3.2). Figure 3.1 shows how college costs have changed relative to grant aid, with both sets of numbers indexed so that their academic year 1970-71 values equal 100. The grant index was below the index for college costs in the 1960s but then rose noticeably above the cost index in the 1970s, suggesting that the burden of paying costs was shifting from families to the providers of grant assistance. Growth in federal grant programmes was largely responsible for this change. In the 1980s, however, the burden of paying for college shifted back towards students and parents, as the grant index fell relative to costs of attendance. Here again, changes in federal grant aid were the primary culprit; we saw earlier that state and institutional grants grew in the 1980s as federal grants languished but could not make up for all the losses in aid from Washington.

Figure 3.2 provides another view of this shifting burden, this time focusing on student loans. Parallel growth in the indexes for loan availability and college costs in the early-to-mid 1970s suggest that the student share of college expenses was staying about stable. Then in the late 1970s, after passage of the Middle Income Student Assistance Act, the loan index started growing much faster than the cost index. Since grant aid had not yet begun to slow, this suggests that student borrowing may have been undertaken in part to reduce the burden on parents, for at least a few years. More recently, with grant aid languishing and with eligibility restrictions in GSL limiting its use as a replacement for the parental contribution, the growing disparity between the loan and cost indexes indicates that students rather than parents or taxpayers are assuming more responsibility for paying college bills.

Figure 3.3 provides a different view of shifting burdens, showing how the proportions of aid provided as grants, loans and work have changed over the years. Grants, which accounted for 66 per cent of all aid in 1970-71 and 80 per cent in 1975-76, fell to 47 per cent of the total

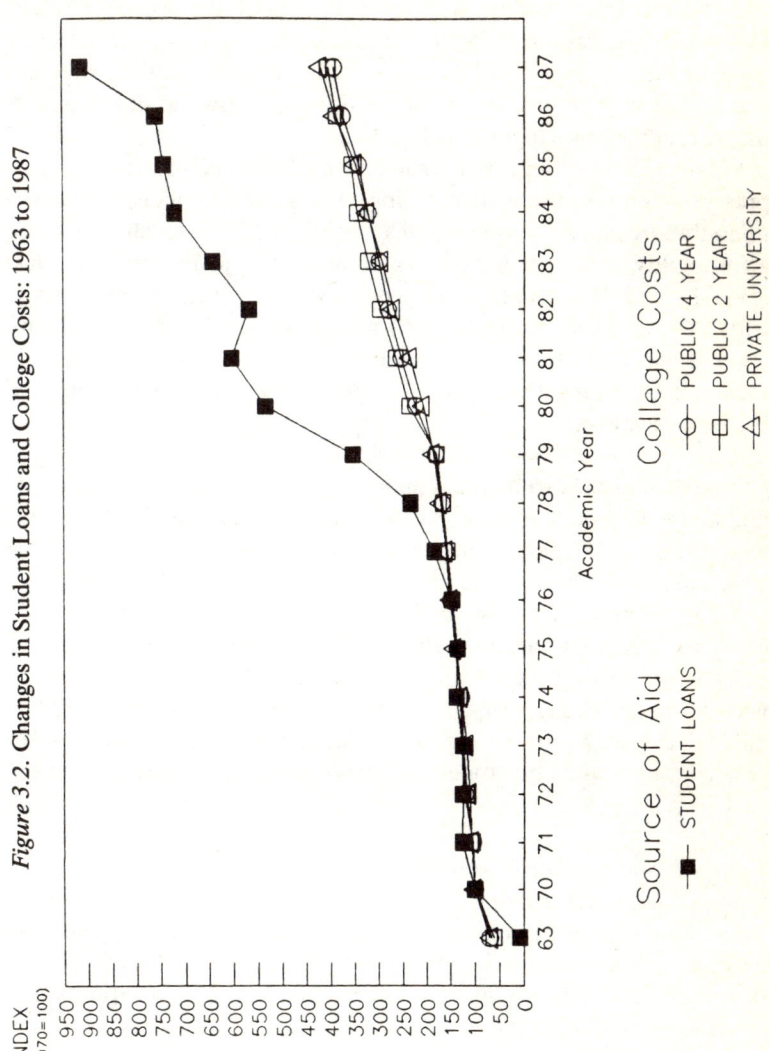

Figure 3.2. Changes in Student Loans and College Costs: 1963 to 1987

in 1987-88. Loans fell from 29 per cent of all aid in 1970-71 to 17 per cent in 1975-76 and then grew steadily, reaching 50 per cent last year.

The picture given of student work effort in Figure 3.3 is misleading, since it captures only the work paid for under the federal College Work-Study Program. A number of states have work-study programmes of their own, and many students hold jobs that are not counted as student aid. We do not really know how the share of costs met through employment has changed.

Finally, Figure 3.4 provides some visual evidence of the increasing pressures felt by parents in meeting their share of college costs, and undoubtedly helps explain why rising tuition levels and the affordability of college have become major political issues in the last several years. It shows that college costs and incomes (both indexed with 1970 levels set equal to 100) rose at about the same rate until about 1980, when they suddenly diverged. Since 1980 family income increases have lagged behind the growth in expenses in all sectors of higher education.

Concerns about US student aid policy

Unlike the United Kingdom, Australia and Sweden, the United States is not now considering major reforms in its student assistance programmes. One reason is that federal programmes, which account for 75 per cent of all aid awarded to students, are reauthorized roughly every five years and are not scheduled to be reviewed again until the early 1990s. Perhaps more importantly, there is no consensus on the need for major changes or agreement on what modifications should be made. Nevertheless, a number of serious questions have been raised in recent years about the student aid system that has evolved over the past 30 years.

The goals and funding of student aid

One consequence of the evolutionary development of American student aid is that the goals of the system are murky. In the 1980s the Reagan Administration challenged federal assistance programmes on the grounds that they had not equalized educational opportunity and that they often benefited institutions rather than students. Does the failure to make much progress toward equalizing opportunity mean that federal programmes have 'failed'? Is it bad if student aid helps institutions as well?

Economist Michael McPherson (1987) has recently suggested an analytical framework for assessing student aid that can help answer these questions. Based on both explicit programme objectives and the

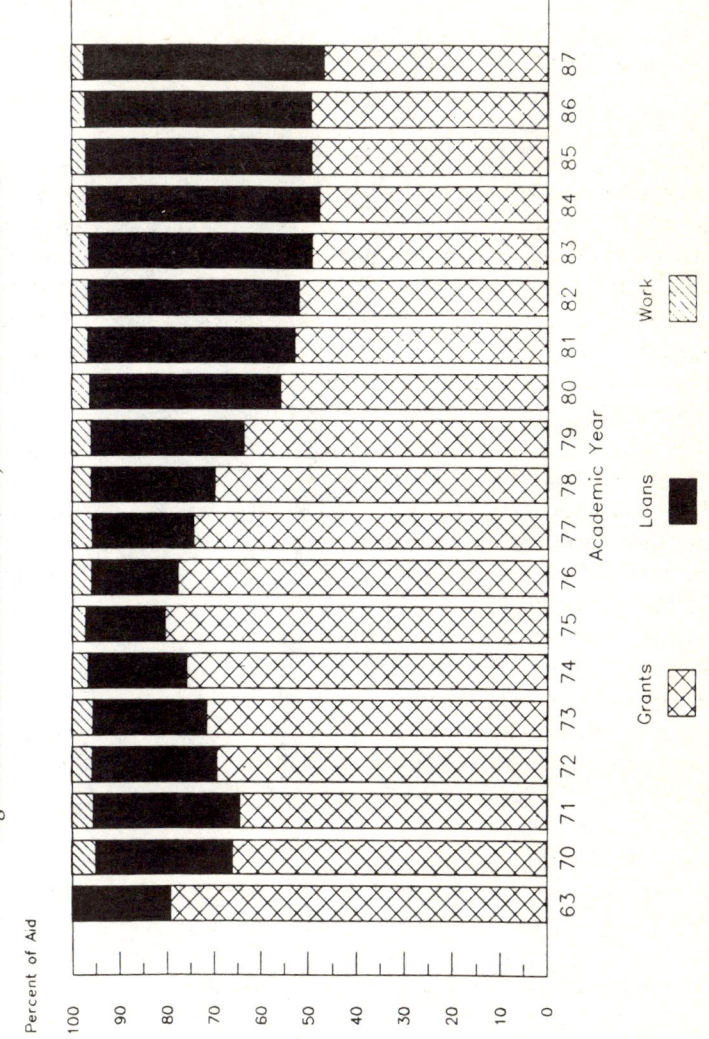

Figure 3.3. Aid Awarded as Grants, Loans and Work: 1963 to 1987

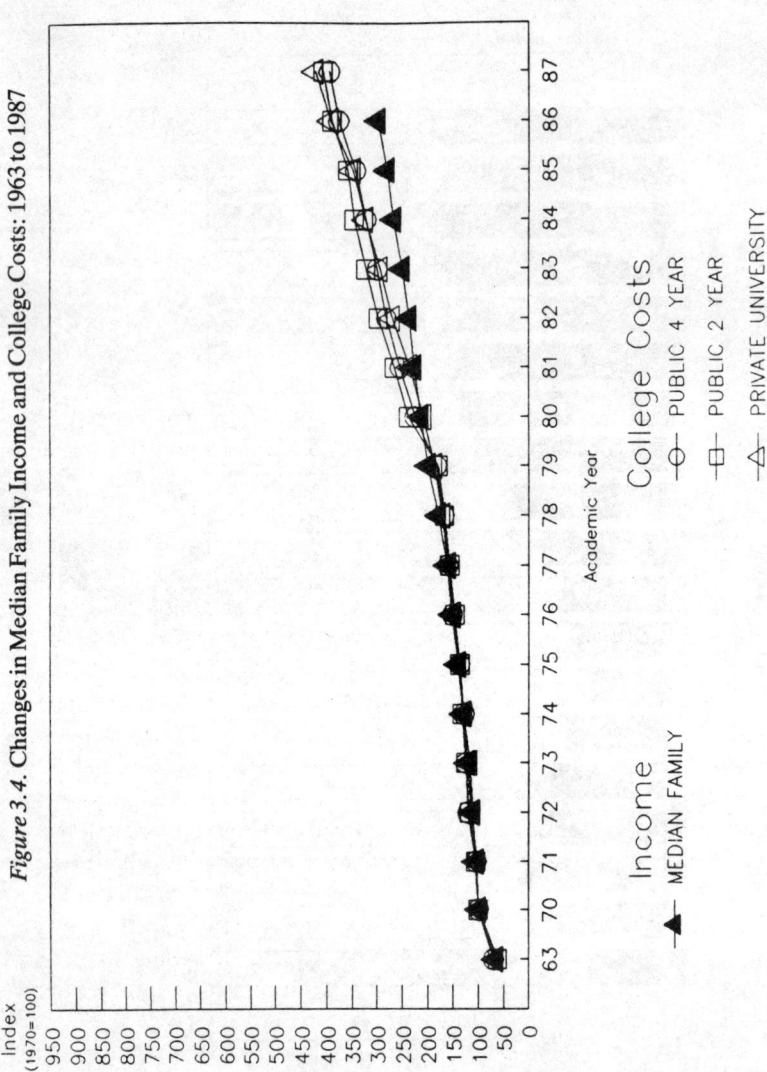

Figure 3.4. Changes in Median Family Income and College Costs: 1963 to 1987

legislative record of their enactment, he argues that federal student aid has three major purposes: equalizing educational opportunity; making the sharing of higher education's costs and benefits fairer; and making higher education institutions work better by making them financially more secure.

Equalizing opportunity was the explicit rationale for the creation of most federal student aid. It is a difficult objective to measure, however, and an even more difficult objective to achieve. An important realization has resulted from recent scrutiny of our progress toward this goal: student aid is not sufficient by itself to reach traditionally-underserved populations. Too many students are lost well before college becomes a real possibility. They either drop out of school altogether or make academic choices that leave them educationally unprepared for higher education. Increasing interest is being expressed in 'early intervention' programmes aimed at 12-to-14 year olds and in programmes like New York State's recently-enacted Liberty Scholarships that offer guarantees of financial support for college many years in advance.

McPherson's framework reminds us that there are other grounds in addition to opportunity on which to measure the success of student aid. Greater fairness in the distribution of costs and benefits might be achieved among those students who do enrol even if the record of expanding opportunity to underserved groups is mixed. Institutional effectiveness might be enhanced by federal support, but that support might be most efficiently given through a market mechansism; i.e. through students choosing which college to attend. In fact, the legislative debates that took place in Congress in 1972 over the provision of institutional or student aid, debates that resulted in the creation of the Pell Grant programme, indicated that institutional support was indeed seen as a legitimate by-product of student aid.

Despite concerns that students may have been given disproportionate influence over higher education because of their buying power, student aid rather than institutional aid continues to be the preferred vehicle for federal support.

Another major issue raised by the imprecise goals of student aid is 'how much is enough'? This question has become more pressing as student aid funding has languished in the 1980s. Aid supporters call for increased funding but are able to offer little in the way of standards for determining how much more aid is needed. In the late 1960s the Carnegie Commission made a proposal that took into account the diversity of student aid programmes and the existence of both state-supported and private institutions, with their very different prices. The Commission suggested that Pell Grants along with the parental contribution should meet the living expenses of students, which are fairly uniform across sectors. Other student aid, especially an augmented state grant programme, should focus on tuition. This plan was not adopted; it envisioned a large increase in state aid that never happened, and it left in state hands more responsibility for equalizing tuition levels between public and private colleges than many private college representatives could accept. Thus student aid continues to come mostly from federal programmes with overlapping objectives and with no benchmarks for measuring the adequacy of funding.

The balance between grants and loans

As earlier comments have indicated, student loans have grown dramatically and now represent half of all financial aid, up from under 20 per cent in the mid-1970s. This had led to numerous calls for 'righting the balance' between grant and loan programmes, especially at the federal level.

Given the diversity of American higher education and its costs to students, and considering the absence of benchmarks noted above, the question of what the right balance between loan and grant funding should be is more a matter of perception than of precise numbers. There is a widespread uneasiness, however, about the disproportionate growth rates in the two kinds of aid. We are concerned that loans, even when subsidized, are less effective than grants in inducing minority and low-income students to enrol in college and that our equal opportunity goal is therefore threatened by the changes of the last decade. We also worry about the negative effects of heavy borrowing on individual students, which will be explored more thoroughly below.

A related issue has to do with the appropriate balance of grants and loans for students at different educational levels. The American post-secondary system is a comparatively open one, and access is wide relative to other nations. We believe in giving almost everyone a shot at some kind of education beyond high school. One consequence of widespread access is that retention is low; many students do not complete full programmes of study. Since student loans are often justified as ways for individuals to invest in their own futures, it becomes appropriate to ask in our context whether loans are an appropriate financing vehicle for all students. Perhaps borrowing should be restricted to students who have completed a year or two of post-secondary study and are therefore likely to finish the programme and reap the economic benefits. This suggests an appealing rationale for providing grants rather than loans to first- and perhaps second-year students. Economic realities, and the difficulties of fitting proprietary (profit-making, often short-term trade) schools into this framework, limit the chances of refocusing aid in this way.

Finally, the changing grant–loan balance raises interesting questions of inter-generational equity between taxpayers and students. Grants are a commitment from this generation of taxpayers to the education of the next generation; loans require today's students to take care of themselves (except to the extent loans are subsidized). We are beginning to wonder, in student aid as in other aspects of American economic life, whether our increasing reliance on loans involves a disproportionate shift in financial responsibilities from today's taxpayers to tomorrow's. To the extent that students borrow because parents cannot or will not contribute as much as they used to, similar questions arise about inter-generational shifts between parents and children.

Student loans: benefits and costs to taxpayers
The great advantage of student loans from the taxpayer's point of view is that they offer 'more bang for the buck'. That is, the funds appropriated as subsidies for loans make available far more dollars in aid than do appropriations for outright grants.

This leveraging effect of student loans is especially apparent in the United States, because we have chosen to rely on private markets rather than government sources for loan capital. Banks are the primary lenders in the GSL Program. State-designated guarantee agencies insure the loans against default and in turn receive reinsurance from the federal government. Washington also pays the interest on student loans while the borrower remains in college and subsidizes the interest rate (through a so-called 'special allowance' to lenders) as long as the loan is in repayment. The special allowance keeps the interest charge to the student borrower at below-market rates while providing the competitive returns banks demand to remain in the programme.

Two aspects of this arrangement have proved problematic: the subsidies and our reliance on private capital markets.

GSL actually contains three types of subsidy: the guarantee against default; the in-college interest payment; and the special allowance. The default guarantee is generally believed to be essential to a programme that relies on private capital markets, since students borrowing to pay for education are not obtaining a tangible asset that can be repossessed in case of non-payment. The cost of this guarantee has become controversial, a point that will be discussed in the next section, and there is talk of reducing the bank's insurance from 100 per cent to 90 per cent to encourage due diligence in loan collection. But there seems to be no feasible alternative to the guarantee at some substantial level. Similarly pragmatic reasons favour the in-college subsidy. A financially-needy student presumably does not have the resources to pay interest or interest-and-principal until he or she finishes or leaves college and enters the workforce.

The really troublesome subsidy is the special allowance. It makes the GLS Program extremely volatile in terms of federal costs and therefore makes the whole programme politically vulnerable when interest rates in the economy rise. Borrowers pay a fixed interest rate, currently 8 per cent. Lenders receive a total return equal to the 91-day Treasury bill rate plus 3¼ per cent. The difference between the total return and the rate charged to borrowers is the special allowance rate. When interest rates in the economy skyrocketed in the early 1980s, so did the special allowance and therefore GSL costs. While concern about this problem has abated as interest rates have fallen, it remains an even more dangerous threat as the federal government tries to bring spending under control. The fear is that an unexpected surge in mandatory spending for GSL subsidies will threaten federal funding for grant programmes.

In a time of fiscal austerity, the fact that we subsidize borrowing through the special allowance also forces us to limit who can borrow in ways that may not be desirable. If the idea that student borrowing represents an investment in one's own future has merit, then it makes sense for all students to have access to loans, not just those whose family circumstances now cause them to qualify as financially needy. Our abortive experience with the Middle Income Student Assistance Act made it clear that we cannot afford to give access to subsidized loans to all comers, however. We therefore feel forced to limit borrowing because our programme mixes loans (which theoretically are logical for all students) with subsidies (which we want to restrict to the financially needy).

Finally, our use of private markets rather than goverment credit to provide loan capital has pluses and minuses. Our spending deficit would be even worse than it is if student loans were 'on budget'. Moreover, American financial institutions provide convenient access to billions of loan dollars annually, and secondary markets have evolved as efficient and sometimes innovative intermediaries between lending institutions and world-wide capital markets.

The question about these accomplishments is: at what cost to the taxpayers? GSL critics argue that the programme provides banks with a riskless and extremely profitable product; lenders claim that student loans are expensive to administer and offer narrow profit margins. Despite our elaborate private market structure, in fact no market mechanism is operating. Since both interest rates to borrowers and returns to lenders are fixed, we are not capturing the presumed efficiencies of a marketplace. In addition, we hide the true costs of the programme from ourselves by not recording future government liabilities incurred when loan commitments are made. Finally, heavy marketing of GSLs by competing banks may encourage students to take on more debt than they otherwise would.

Loans: benefits and costs to borrowers

The chief benefit of loans to students is the same as the chief benefit to taxpayers: leverage. The existence of loans give students wider access to financial assistance than would be possible if the aid were in the form of outright, non-repayable grants. Even if we were to double our spending on Pell Grants, for (a far-fetched) example, it would replace less than half of the over $10 billion students now borrow each year. Fiscal realities demand that we continue to rely on loans as a major source of funding for students in post-secondary education.

Two major concerns are frequently expressed about our reliance on loans as a major financing tool: excessive debt burdens and high default rates. Both issues are probably more confused than clarified by the highly-politicized debates over them.

The recent and rapid increase in student borrowing has led to fears that students are becoming excessively indebted. Such fears are compounded by the high levels of debt that a borrower could theoretically accumulate by taking out the maximum loan in every available programme, by large increases in maximum loan levels enacted in 1986, and by stories in the popular press about students with $50,000 or $100,000 in educational debt. (The fact that such students are usually doctors with high earning potential and little concern about their ability to repay tends to go unnoticed.) Attention to the issue is important, since we are in uncharted territory; never have young people been asked or permitted to undertake such long-term financial obligations. Facts are few; in this as in other aspects of student aid we are unable to answer basic questions, such as how much debt the typical borrower has upon college graduation or about how many students are borrowing at high levels. In this area, too, we have failed to establish benchmarks, such as percentages of income that must be devoted to loan repayment, that would help us determine when we are approaching danger. Studies of manageable debt burdens, for example, have ranged in their recommendations from 3 to 15 per cent of income, hardly useful for policy purposes even if we had better information on what percentage of income student borrowers are devoting to loan repayment.

Nevertheless, the data we do have suggest that borrowing is not out of control and that most student borrowers have quite manageable debt burdens. In addition, borrowers report that loans play a critical part in their ability to finance higher education. Despite fears about creating 'negative dowries', loans have clearly not discouraged the enrolment of women, who now represent a majority of college students in the United States. We are less certain about minorities; many feel that increasing reliance on loan financing has contribtuted to the stagnation and perhaps even decline of minority enrolments in the 1980s.

Though debt burden worries currently seem unwarranted, at least for most borrowers, our loan programmes do expose students to risks that could be reduced or eliminated. In particular, we do a relatively poor job, compared to some other nations, in protecting our student borrowers against the risk that their educational investment will not in fact 'pay off'. Except for a temporary reprieve from loan repayment in the event of unemployment, we do not provide students with insurance against excessive debt burdens due to low income or other unexpected turns of fate.

Our failure to protect borrowers in this way contributes to a default rate of about 14 per cent, or 10 after accounting for eventual collection of postponed repayments. Student loan defaults have become a major political issue in Washington in the past year, because they now cost the federal government over $1.5 billion annually. It is important to recognize, however, that while default costs have skyrocketed, the default *rate* has increased only a little. Our newly-discovered default 'problem' stems from the large increase in borrowing, leading to larger amounts of debt coming into repayment. It is not the result of a growing unwillingness to repay student loans.

In fact, the evidence about who fails to repay and why indicates that it is not the large borrowers who default, but rather, students with relatively small debts who *cannot* repay. Defaulters are found disproportionately among students who are enrolled in relatively short-term programmes, students who drop out without completing degrees or receiving the intended credential, borrowers who take out only one loan, and people with low incomes. These are precisely the individuals who might be protected by some kind of low-income insurance, or by different student aid policies that emphasized grant assistance to students until they become academically established. Thus our default rate and our default 'problem' result in part from the way we design an administer our student loan programmes.

Complexity
The US system of student aid, if one can call it a system, is incredibly complex. The multiplicity of programmes and sponsors reflects our federal system and our diversified responsibility for providing and financing higher education. The costs and benefits of this unique structure offer less to instruct the international community than other aspects of our student aid policies. Nevertheless, complexity should not go unmentioned, since it is one of our major concerns.

One aspect of this issue *is* relevant to countries having or considering aid policies built on both grants and loans. An important question, if the programmes are need-based, is whether to assess need the same way for both types of aid. Assessing need differently in different programmes is confusing for parents and students; but it makes a student aid system more flexible.

Until recently, we used more stringent criteria in assessing need for grants than for loans. Grant eligibility depends on a fairly complicated review of both income and assets. Before 1979, students could borrow under GSL so long as their family incomes fell below a specified level, which was raised over the years until nearly everyone qualified. This was one of the arguments for eliminating income considerations altogether in the late 1970s, to simplify programme administration. When a need test was reimposed in the 1980s, students from families above a designated income level were required to go through a more detailed need determination, but the required assessment did not have to include parental assets. Not only was this test simpler than the one used for grants, but disregarding assets makes some sense in a loan programme. It leaves to the family the decision about whether to borrow for college or to cash in some of those assets instead.

The trouble comes, here as elsewhere, from our practice of mixing up subsidies (or indirect grants) in the loan programme. Because of these subsidies, we feel the programme has to be restricted to the truly needy, and this determination needs to be made in a detailed manner. In 1987-88, we began requiring 'full' need analysis (including a review of assets) of all borrowers. Thus our policies again constrain us, making administration of loans more complicated than it might be.

The role of parents
The final issue I want to raise about burden-sharing in the United States has to do with the role of parents. I noted earlier that our system of financing the expenses of college is built on the assumption that parents and students will in the first instance provide what they can. Need-based student aid is provided to bridge the gap between what parents and students can afford and what college costs.

The assumption of parental responsiblity has become more tenuous as our student population has changed. Many adults now enrol in higher education, as well as younger students who have been on their own financially and do not wish to be dependent on their parents. Ensuring equity in the treatment of different types of students has become more difficult, and the question of how to define a financially independent student has become a constant question on the political agenda. Our current definition, which we would recommend to no one, requires 11 questions on the financial aid form and is almost certain to be changed (again) at the next legislative opportunity because it is so difficult to administer.

Despite these difficulties, however, parental responsibility remains key to our financing policies. Increasingly, as we come to grips with our broader fiscal difficulties, we recognize how important it is that we use scarce student aid dollars for those who truly cannot afford to pay for college on their own. The corollary is that those who can pay must be encouraged to do so. If student aid discourages families from saving ahead, because of the 'tax' on assets, then perhaps there should be explicit savings incentives as well as student aid.

Encouraging families to plan ahead for college expenses – either through so-called 'tuition futures' or more conventional savings plans – has been the hot topic in higher education finance in the past two years. Tuition futures, a kind of pre-payment contract, were enacted by the state of Michigan late in 1986 and quickly became a legislative fad. Several more states have enacted plans, though financial and administrative complexities and questions have slowed implementation. Many other states have enacted tax-favoured savings plans, and in 1988 both presidential candidates endorsed a federally-subsidized savings vehicle. Many observers question the efficacy of tax subsidies for savings and fear that their popularity has or will divert attention from the more pressing need of families without the resources to save. Nevertheless, it appears that the savings incentive issue will have a prominent place on the legislative agenda for a while longer.

Conclusion: some propositions about burden sharing and student aid
To summarize this review of the American experience with sharing the burdens of paying for college, let me offer several concluding propositions that might serve as the basis for additional discussion:

- burden-sharing among parents, students, taxpayers and institutions/philanthropists works, at least in our context;
- student aid alone is not a panacea for the problem of unequal access to higher education;
- explicit policy goals are necessary if there is to be a meaningful debate on the questions 'how much is enough?' and 'what is the proper balance between grant and loan financing?';
- up to a point, student loans increase the financial resources available to pay for college without deleterious effects on borrowers;
- issues of access to and adminstration of a student loan programme will be easier to resolve if the provision of subsidies can be kept separate from the provision of loans;
- the costs of a student loan programme can become problematic if they are volatile, or if they are imprecisely recorded in current financial accounts;
- the magnitude of default rates in student loan programmes depends in part on how the programmes are designed and administered;
- low-income 'insurance' could protect students from many of the risks of borrowing to pay for college;
- in designing student aid programmes, there is an important trade-off to consider between minimizing complexity of administration and maximising flexibility in meeting student needs;
- all of the potential partners need to share the burdens of college financing if access to education is to grow;
- monitoring of how the burdens of paying for college are shared and are shifting requires better data collection than we in the United States historically have performed.

Notes
1. In 1958 the loans were called National Defense Student Loans, but were later renamed National Direct Student Loans (NDSL), and are now called Perkins Loans, in honour of the former Senator Carl D Perkins.

2. Throughout this chapter figures are given in US dollars only.

References

Johnstone, D. B. (1986), *Sharing the Costs of Higher Education: student financial assistance in the United Kingdom, the Federal Republic of Germany, France, Sweden and the United States.* New York: College Entrance Examination Board.

McPherson, M. (1987), *How Can We Tell if Federal Student Aid is Working?* New York: College Entrance Examination Board.

Chapter Four

International Experience of Financial Support for Students: Recent Trends and Developments

Maureen Woodhall

Sharing the costs of higher education

Some years ago the Carnegie Commission in the United States published a study entitled *Higher Education: Who benefits? Who pays? Who should pay?* Although economists have made valiant efforts to answer the first question, no one now believes that the answer to 'who should pay' can be derived purely from an analysis of the distribution of benefits. Higher education benefits both the individual and society and in all countries both the individual and the taxpayer share the costs, though as Bruce Johnstone demonstrates in Chapter 2 the burdens are shared in very different proportions in different countries.

At present, a number of countries, including Britain, are engaged in re-examining the question of 'who should pay?' and have introduced, or proposed, new methods of sharing the costs of higher education between the main financing partners: students, parents and taxpayers. Some countries are also trying to develop the role of a fourth partner. In the United States, as Bruce Johnstone observes, philanthropy – both individual and institutional – is an important source of finance, particularly for private universities. This is also important in some other countries with a strong private sector of higher education – notably Japan – and some people believe that it could be much more significant in this country if the tax system provided more incentives for institutional donations, as in the United States, or if universities made more efforts to attract endowment income, as some have recently begun to do.

Many people have argued that industry should be regarded as the fourth partner, and should play a much more direct role in financing higher education, since employers share in the benefits of higher productivity from graduates in the labour market and from the application of research. Some countries are trying to increase the contribution of industry, and have suggested some form of education tax or levy, or industrial sponsorship of students. In Australia, for example, the Committee on Higher Education Funding which reported in 1988 recommended that a tripartite body be established to develop education and training levy arrangements in industry, and that other initiatives be explored to attract and increase industry support for higher education. However, as Bruce Johnstone argues, industry 'is not an ultimate bearer of costs in the manner of students, parents, taxpayers and donors, but is rather an intermediary that in turn passes the costs on to consumers, employees, general taxpayers or stockholders'(Chapter 2, p.28). Nevertheless this role of intermediary may be important; Johnstone recognizes that 'Business remains a potentially significant player in that it can support higher education to an extent that the ultimate bearers of this burden – i.e. the consumers – might not voluntarily choose to do' (p.28).

Several countries are therefore exploring ways of increasing the contribution of industry. In the United Kingdom the government has urged universities and polytechnics to seek additional funding from industry, in the form of research contracts, sponsorship or donations, and the Council for Industry and Higher Education is encouraging a wider debate about ways of developing the partnership of government, industry and higher education institutions. This might include greater contributions from industry to student support, and in a paper published in 1988, *Towards a Partnership: supporting more students* the council argues for substantial reforms in the British system of student support, and adds 'if the changes led to increased demand for company sponsorship, we believe companies would accept that as a worthwhile price to pay' (Council for Industry and Higher Education, 1988, p.1).

Shifting the financial burdens

The main changes being introduced or proposed in several countries involve the three main financial partners: students, parents and taxpayers. Bruce Johnstone's comparisons of student support in the United Kingdom, France, the Federal Republic of Germany, Sweden and the United States in 1986 showed that students bear a greater share of the costs of higher education in the United States, through loans and part-time work, than in the other four countries; the parental share is lowest in Sweden, since the student aid system does not assume or require any parental contribution. The taxpayer's contribution is greater in Britain than in the other countries, because of the system of free tuition for the vast majority of British students, combined with maintenance grants and the absence (until now) of student loans.

In the United Kingdom, however, the decline in the real value of the grant in recent years, together with increases in the assessed parental contribution, mean that there has been a shift from taxpayers to parents, which is shown clearly in DES statistics on student awards (see Figure 4.1). But surveys of student income suggest that as many as half of all students who should receive a parental contribution do not receive the full amount (Barr and Low, 1988). This means that although the grants system does not officially require a student contribution, in practice deficiencies in the parental contribution are forcing an increasing number of students to live in poverty or take out bank overdrafts. Thus we already have an unofficial system of student loans.

The introduction of 'top-up loans' as proposed in the White Paper in November 1988, as a result of the government's review of student support (see Chapter 1), would further shift the balance between students, parents and taxpayers. At the same time several other countries, including Australia and Sweden, have announced changes in their system of student support which will shift the financial burdens between students, parents and taxpayers, or change the balance between grants and loans.

So it is clear that the UK is far from being alone in considering how the costs of higher education should be shared, what combination of grants and loans would best achieve the objectives of equality of opportunity and increased participation in higher education without imposing excessive burdens on public expenditure, and whether incremental or radical change is needed in the current system of cost sharing in higher education and financial support for students.

It is not only in the developed countries of Europe, the United States, Japan, Australia and New Zealand that changes in student support systems are on the political agenda. The World Bank has advocated a shift towards greater cost recovery and student loans rather than grants in developing countries (World Bank, 1986) and several governments in Africa and Asia are examining the feasibility of student loans, and in Latin America, where a number of student loan programmes already exist, changes in the system of student support are being considered.

The remainder of this chapter attempts to summarize the main trends and developments that have taken place in recent years in financial support for students in other developed countries, and looks at recent proposals for change in Australia and New Zealand, the Federal Republic of Germany and the United States. More detailed examiniation of American and Swedish experience is provided by Janet Hansen (Chapter 3) and Martin Morris (Chapter 5) and finally Nicholas Barr (Chapter 6) presents an alternative proposal for Britain which he believes would overcome some of the problems and weaknesses that have occurred in other countries.

Recent changes in relative shares of higher education costs
If we examine trends in the share of costs borne by students, parents and taxpayers in most Western countries in the last 25 years, there are certain similarities. In the early 1960s and 1970s the desire to expand higher education and ensure more equal participation by different social groups led to a marked shift in the balance between public and private finance. The taxpayer provided an increasing proportion of the funds for higher education in most countries as a result of either abolition or reduction of tuition fees, or the introduction of new forms of student support, including grants, loans, subsidized job opportunities in the US, through the federally subsidized College Work-Study programme, or indirect subsidies, such as the provision of low-cost board and lodgings for students in France and the Federal Republic of Germany.

In the UK, the existing system of mandatory grants was introduced in 1962. Sweden established the present system of study means (*studie medel*) in 1964, and in the US a small student loan programme (the National Defense Student Loan programme) was introduced in 1958, followed by the College Work-Study programme in 1964 and the introduction of Educational Opportunity Grants and the Guaranteed Student Loan programme in 1965. In the Federal Republic of Germany, the Federal Law for the Promotion of Education, popularly know as *BAföG*, introduced a system of student grants which was quickly converted to a combined grants and loans programme. In Australia tuition fees were abolished in 1974, and a new scheme of income support was introduced, the Tertiary Education Award Scheme (TEAS), which was replaced in 1987 by a more generous programme called AUSTUDY. In Japan the Japanese Scholarhip Foundation, which provides financial aid only in the form of loans, grew rapidly in the 1960s, and in the early 1970s a Current Cost Subsidy

Figure 4.1. The rate of grant and average contributions[1,2]

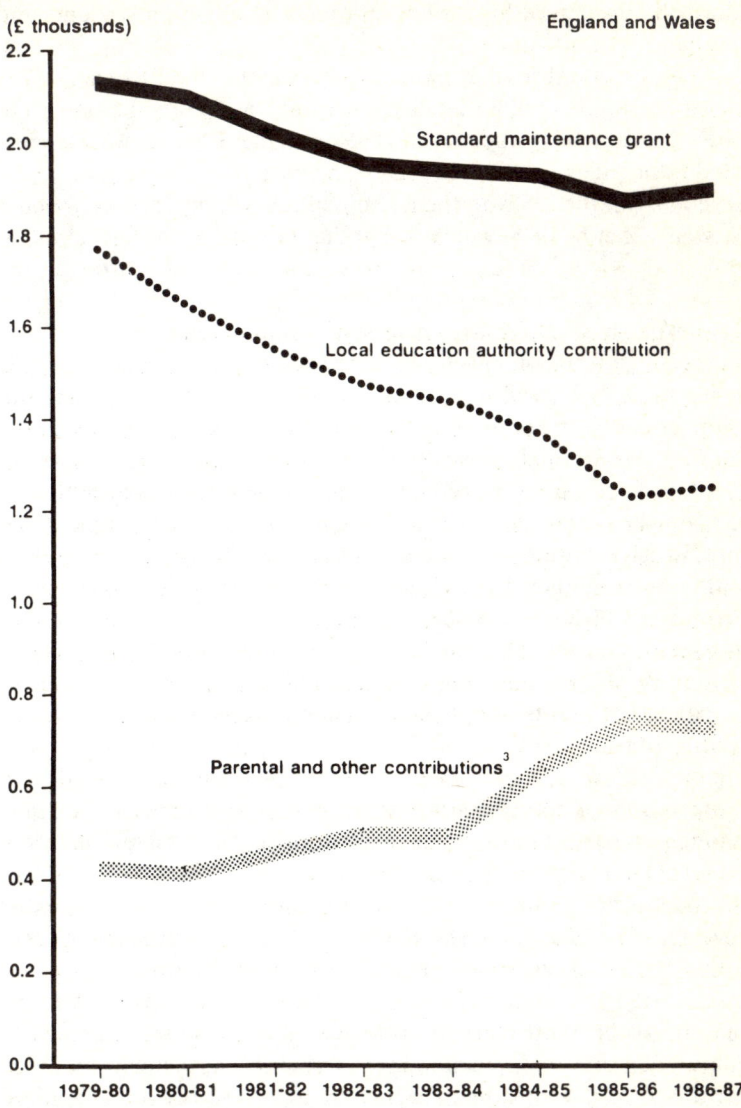

(£ thousands)   **England and Wales**

Standard maintenance grant

Local education authority contribution

Parental and other contributions[3]

1979-80 1980-81 1981-82 1982-83 1983-84 1984-85 1985-86 1986-87

1   At 1986-87 prices, based on the RPI at September of each academic year.

2   Figures for 1983-84 and earlier include a notional amount for excess travel allowances: from 1984-85 onwards provision for travel costs was incorporated within the main rate of grant.

3   Assuming full payment of parental contributions: including notional assessments in respect of minimum award-holders up to 1984-85 and of students for whom fees only were paid by LEAs in 1985-86 and 1986-87

Source: DES Statistical Bulletin 2/89, 'Student awards in England and Wales: 1986-87'.

was introduced, to subsidize tuition costs in private universities, and reduce the burden of higher education costs falling on students and their parents.

So, in most countries there was a marked shift in the 1960s and 1970s towards increased public finance education and a reduction in the share of costs met by students and their parents. Eligibility for means-tested student support was also increased in many countries, particularly in the US with the passing of the Middle Income Student Assistance Act of 1978, which meant that most students had access to subsidized loans, offered by commercial banks through the Guaranteed Student Loan programme.

This trend has been sharply reversed in many countries in the 1980s, and recent and current developments in Australia, Japan and the US, as well as the UK, will further accentuate the trend towards greater contributions from parents and students and reductions in public subsidies. We have already seen, in Figure 4.1, the sharp increase in parental contributions to student awards in the UK and the decline in the taxpayer's share, together with the decline in the real value of the grant, which means that students themselves must bear a greater share of the costs, either by reducing their standard of living or by borrowing, which in the absence of official student loans means either a bank overdraft or use of credit cards. In the United States, as Janet Hansen has shown, there has been an increased reliance on loans, at the expense of grants, which have declined as a proportion of federal student aid from 80 per cent in 1975-76 to 47 per cent in 1987-88.

In the Federal Republic of Germany the *BAföG* system of combined grants and loans was converted to an all-loans programme in 1984, although as Bruce Johnstone has shown, the level of subsidy involved in interest-free loans with repayment spread over twenty years means that there is a very substantial 'hidden grant'. Indeed, in his book he suggested that 'the post-1984 *BAföG*, while certainly shifting some burden from taxpayer to student, in fact shifted very little and has kept most of *BAföG*'s costs, even as a loan programme, a reponsibility in the end, of the West German taxpayer' (Johnstone 1986, p. 53). In Chapter 2 of this book, he therefore comments on 'the political blood that was shed over a student loan programme so heavily subsidized that the true costs are still borne overwhelmingly by the taxpayer' (p. 43). Nevertheless the fact that under the *BAföG* system all student support has been in the form of loans since 1984 has been much criticized in Germany and a Commission set up to review student support has recently (November 1988) recommended that grants should be reintroduced and support should be in the form of 50 per cent grant and 50 per cent loan.

In Japan, the Current Cost Subsidy – which was introduced in the 1970s to reduce the impact on parents of the increased tuition fees in private universities – has declined in real terms, and in the last few years tuition fees in both public and private universities have risen sharply. A recent study for the OECD of the finance of higher education in Japan (OECD, 1988) shows that the ratio of average student charges to GNP per capita fell from 30 per cent in 1965 to 18 per cent in 1975, which represented a significant reduction in the parental burden and an increase in the taxpayer's share. However, between 1976 and 1981 average tuition fees rose by over 50 per cent, while the Current Cost Subsidy rose much more slowly, and in 1982 a government committee recommended that it should be frozen at the existing level. Continued increases in tuition fees mean that the ratio of student charges to GNP per capita is now almost 30 per cent, which is the highest level since 1966. This shift in the financial burden from taxpayers to parents has been accompanied by a shift towards greater contributions from students. In the 1970s the number and value of student loans provided by the Japanese Scholarship Foundation grew, and all the loans were interest-free. In 1984, however, as a result of financial pressure, the government introduced a new form of loans which charge students 3 per cent interest, and students taking high cost courses, such as medicine and dentistry, can apply for supplementary loans at 6.5 per cent.

In Australia a Higher Education Adminstrative Charge was introduced in 1986 and in the spring of 1988 the Wran Committee on Higher Education Funding recommended a 'higher education contribution scheme that is based on users paying a proportion of the costs of their higher education through the tax system'. The original proposals were that all those who enrolled in higher education would immediately incur a tax liability, which would be paid by all those whose income exceeded the average annual earnings of full-time employees. The tax would be set at 2 per cent of taxable income which would be paid until beneficiaries had repaid 20 per cent of the costs of their higher education. The scheme was described as 'tax debit' rather than a 'graduate tax' since all those who have benefited from higher education would become liable, regardless of whether or not they graduate. On the other hand, they would no longer be liable if their income was below the national average, or when they had contributed

20 per cent of the costs of their education – which would vary according to subject, from A$1500 (about £750) a year for arts courses, A$2500 (£1250) a year for science and engineering and A$3000 (£1500) a year for medicine and dentistry. At the same time, the Higher Education Administrative Charge would be abolished.

These proposals have now been slightly modified. The required contribution from every student will be about A$1800 (about £900) per year, regardless of subject, which represents about 20 per cent of the average cost per student. The rate of tax, however, will vary with income level. Former students will begin to pay the tax when their income reaches the level of average annual earnings of A$22,000 (£11,000). At this level of income, they will pay a tax of 1 per cent, which will rise to 2 per cent when their income reaches A$25,000 (£12,500) and 3 per cent when they earn A$35,000 (£17,500) a year. Alternatively, students may pay their contributions as an 'up-front' fee, in which case they will be eligible for a discount of about 15 per cent.

Not surprisingly, this scheme has been attacked by students, but the Committee on Higher Education argued strongly that it would be fairer than the present system of 'free' higher education which disproportionately benefits students from upper income backgrounds, and is largely financed by taxpayers, many of whom have much lower earnings prospects than highly privileged university graduates. The Committee recommended the new tax debit system, to be combined with improvements in the income support provided by AUSTUDY, as 'a funding partnership in which the beneficiaries make a direct and fair contribution to the cost of higher education, to supplement the funds provided by taxpayers, who currently bear over 90 per cent of the total costs. The Committee based its recommendations on the following principles:

- far greater access to higher education by people from financially and other disadvantaged backgrounds is needed – higher education should not continue to be the preserve of the relatively privileged;
- the advantaged who use and benefit directly from higher education ought to contribute more directly to the cost of the system;
- employers and industry also benefit financially and should contribute directly to the cost;
- Australian taxpayers should not be expected to carry the burden of financing the growth envisaged in higher education, particularly since few directly enjoy its financial benefits.

The Committee's insistence that a shift in the financial burden from taxpayers to students or their parents would result in a more equitable system explains why the Australian Labour Party has agreed to the proposals. Recent research in Australia has demonstrated that the abolition of tuition fees and the introduction of income support in 1974 did not lead to increased equality of opportunity. In 1984, 43 per cent of children from professional families entered higher education in Australia, compared with 9 per cent of children from unskilled families, and the Committee quotes a study of trends in participation rates which concluded that

> fee abolition had a marginal effect at best, on the accessibility of higher
> education for socially and economically disadvantaged groups; at worst,
> it provided a further benefit to the economically advantaged.
> (Committee on Higher Education Funding, 1988, p.5)

Some months after the publication of the Wran Committee report in Australia a similar proposal was put forward in New Zealand by a Working Group on Post-Compulsory Education and Training. The chairman of the Working Group, Professor Hawke, advocated greater reliance on private funding for post-compulsory education on the grounds that it is an investment offering a high private rate of return:

> I draw a parallel between students and dairy farmers in nineteenth-
> century New Zealand. Many of the latter experienced hardship as they
> developed their farms. They later benefited from assets of vastly
> increased value. There was little case for public support of the farmers
> who chose to receive income in the form of higher property values,
> tolerating subsistence living for some years in return for the prospect of
> wealth later. (Hawke, 1988, p.28).

The Hawke report therefore proposed a system of fees which would increase resources for higher education institutions by something like 20 per cent, together with a system of government loans for students, with income-contingent repayments collected through the tax system. As in Australia, this shift in the balance between public and private funding was advocated on grounds of equity, and Hawke argued that assistance for disadvantaged groups should be provided by remission of fees for particular types of course, such as 'access' or 'bridging' courses which cater particularly for groups which are under-represented in higher education, such as women and ethnic minorities.

Both the Wran and the Hawke reports challenged the belief that the costs of higher education should be overwhelmingly borne by taxpayers, and the Wran Committee cited evidence to show that providing free education had not ensured equality of opportunity. Similar doubts have been expressed in other countries about the effects of increased public subsidies in the 1970s. In the US, Lee Hansen has argued that the considerable increase in federal government expenditure on grants and loans in the 1970s largely benefited middle-income, rather than lower-income students (Hansen, 1983). In Sweden, a study of the influence of student aid on the participation rate of different social groups concluded that when the system of study means was first introduced in the 1960s 'it had a significant socially equalizing effect, an effect which has now been lost' (Reuterberg and Svensson, 1987). Partly as a result of the growing concern that the Swedish system of combined grants and loans was no longer achieving its objective of equalizing opportunities for higher education, major changes were introduced in 1989. These changes are examined in more detail in the chapter by Martin Morris (Chapter 5). One of the main changes is that the balance between grants and loans will be changed. In future, students will receive a higher proportion of their total study assistance as a grant, but at the same time the terms of repayment of loans will be less generous. The net effect of these changes will be that there will be very little change in the relative contributions of students and taxpayers, but the incidence of the subsidies will alter. Students will receive higher subsidies while they are actually studying and lower subsidies in the form of interest reductions after they graduate. In other words, what Bruce Johnstone calls the 'hidden grant' will become an explicit grant, and the interest charged on student loans will be much closer to market rates.

A similar trend towards higher interest on student loans can be observed in other countries. There are now two kinds of loans available in Japan: interest-free loans for low-income students and loans with interest for those from higher-income families. In the United States there are at least three different rates of interest on student loans. The most highly subsidized – Perkins loans – are reserved for low-income students; the Guaranteed Student Loans programme charges higher interest and parents who borrow under the most recently established programme – PLUS (Parent Loans for Undergraduate Students) – pay interest which is close to market rates. In her chapter Janet Hansen recommends that in future the provision of subsidies for financially needy students should be kept separate from the provision of loans, which could be available at market rates to all who want to borrow to finance higher education.

Another change in the Swedish system is that in future loan

repayments will be linked to income; graduates will be required to pay 4 per cent of their income as loan repayments, until the loan is repaid. At present loan repayments are not dependent on income, but graduates must repay their loan by the age of 50. This change has been introduced because of concern in Sweden about the increasing burden of debt. This concern is shared in other countries, particularly the United States. Janet Hansen's chapter points out that research in the US suggests that borrowing is not out of control, and that most student borrowers have manageable debt burdens. However, she also emphasizes that there is no consensus about what constitutes a 'manageable debt'. Different studies have ranged in their recommendations from 3 to 15 per cent of income. It is interesting to note that both Australia and Sweden have proposed income-contingent loan repayments; Australia will require 2 per cent, or 3 per cent from those with high incomes, whereas Sweden requires 4 per cent of graduate income. However, some recent proposals for income-contingent loans in the US, summarized below, have considered 9 or even 10 per cent as a reasonable proportion.

Recent proposals for change in the United States
In the United States there is continuing debate about the effects of the uniquely complex system of financial support for students. Although as Janet Hansen points out in her chapter, the United States is not currently considering major reforms in its student assistance programmes, since federal student support programmes are not due to be reauthorized until the early 1990s, there have been a number of important changes in recent years, and a number of issues are currently being debated. Indeed, the subject of student aid is never far from the political agenda in the US, and there are frequent proposals for change or attempts to introduce some new kind of programme, such as the experimental Income Contingent Loans introduced on a small scale a few years ago, or Michigan State's 'prepayment plan' which encourages parents to begin saving for their children's higher education as soon as they are born.

Thus Lawrence Gladieux, director of the Washington Office of the College Board, has described student aid as 'a hot issue at the moment in the US' (Gladieux, 1989). It even appeared briefly in the 1988 presidential campaign, when Michael Dukakis was reported to be considering a proposal for a radical reform of federal student loans, along the lines of Australia's proposed graduate tax. Several such proposals have been made in the US, including the so-called Zacharias

Plan in 1967, which proposed an Educational Opportunity Bank which would lend money for higher education to students who would promise to pay a fixed proportion of their earnings once they started work. A similar idea was put forward in the 1970s by John Silber of Boston University, who proposed a Tuition Advance Fund to provide income-contingent loans. Now the idea has re-emerged with a proposal by Robert Reischauer of the Brookings Institution for a new Higher Education Loan Program, which would at least have a more appealing acronym – HELP – than the Auxiliary Loans to Assist Students, which were introduced in 1981, with the unfortunate acronym ALAS.

As the new Bush Adminstration in the US prepares to tackle the budget deficit and the need to reauthorize the Higher Education Act in 1991, the College Board has recently defined the question facing Congress as one of deciding 'whether to consider fundamental restructuring or continue a pattern of stop-gap changes and quick-fix cost reductions under pressure' (College Board, 1989). To help explore this question, the College Board organized a seminar in 1988 on student loan policy alternatives, which examined a number of proposals ranging from radical reform to incremental change. (Gladieux, 1989)

Among the radical reforms suggested were two proposals that have much in common with Nicholas Barr's proposal for student loans based on the National Insurance system. Robert Reischauer has proposed a new Higher Education Loan Programme (HELP) based on a social insurance approach. All students (regardless of income) would be entitled to borrow from a higher education trust fund and would repay the loan through the social security tax system, by means of a constant percentage throughout working life. Reischauer estimates that a payroll tax of 0.24 per cent per $1,000 borrowed would be sufficient for each cohort of borrowers to repay their loans in full, but this would mean that those who were unemployed, or had low-paid jobs, might never pay enough tax to repay their loan in full, whereas those with high earnings might repay their loan several times over. Thus, there would be an element of redistribution of financial burdens of graduates, with high earners subsidizing the low paid, and Reischauer justifies this on the grounds that those with high earnings benefit more from the loans than those with low earnings. The degree of redistribution is limited, however, by the fact that social security taxes are not levied on earnings above a certain maximum ($45,000 in 1988).

The scheme would also involve a redistribution of financial burdens from parents, who under current arrangements are expected to contribute to their children's higher education expenses unless they have low incomes, to students, who would pay additional social insurance contribution throughout their working lives. Reischauer believes that this is necessary in the contemporary United States, because of changing family patterns. Rising rates of separation, divorce and illegitimate births mean that

> over half of the children born in 1980 will not be living with both of their biological parents by the time they reach college age . . . In the end, it may be impossible to design a truly equitable mechanism for determining the amount a family should be expected to contribute to its child's education. It may be equally difficult to design a test that can fairly determine whether a student is truly financially dependent. (Reischauer, in Gladieux, 1989,p.39)

Therefore HELP, which its advocate believes is a 'student loan programme for the twenty-first century', would avoid the problem by treating *all* students as financially independent – as the Swedish system already does.

William Byron has proposed what he calls a variation on the time-honoured American practice of 'working your way through college', in this case 'college first, work later'. His proposal is for a Federal Revolving Fund which would provide students with an advance to be repaid through the income tax system. Once again, repayment would be income contingent, and based on a fixed percentage of earnings, but unlike the HELP proposal, this tax would be paid only until the loan was fully repaid. It would not represent a life time commitment to pay a graduate tax. Byron's proposal draws on earlier proposals for income-contingent loans and a revolving fund. The first such proposal was made by Milton Friedman in 1945 and later elaborated in the 1960s (Friedman, 1962). Later proposals included the Zacharias plan in 1967, to set up an Educational Opportunity Bank to provide income-contingent loans and John Silber's proposal for a Tuition Advance Fund, put forward in the 1970s. None of these proposals was put into effect, but Byron believes that the time has come for a reappraisal of this idea.

Among those who reject the case for radical reform are several economists and student aid administrators who argue that relatively minor changes to existing loan programmes would be sufficient to overcome problems such as default or the high cost to the federal government of providing interest subsidies and a special allowance to lenders. Joseph Cronin, President of the Massachusetts Higher

Education Assistance Corporation, believes that the Guaranteed Student Loans Program is one of the great success stories of American higher education and argues that

> Hundreds of parents have told this writer 'we could not have paid those college bills without the GSL Program'. Thus what critics originally described as a 'loan of convenience for the middle class has become a staple, a necessity for millions of families each year. (Cronin in Gladieux, 1989, p.57)

He proposes relatively modest changes, including an increase in the maximum loan limits of the GSL and steps to reduce defaults. He denies that student loan debts are excessive, quoting surveys which show that most students report that their debt burden is not excessive and a few say that they wish they had borrowed more. He also quotes studies by the National Commission on Student Financial Aid which show that 'the more student loan debt a borrower acquires, the less likely the borrower is to default'. On the other hand, those who are most likely to default are students from private vocational schools, often with small debts, but who are subsequently unemployed. He therefore proposes an increase in grants and scholarships for low-income students and for those taking courses leading to health care and social service professions, who are unlikely to have high earnings.

Arthur Hauptman has proposed rather more fundamental changes to existing loan programmes, including a low-income insurance fund to allow borrowers with low earnings to defer repayment, and graduated repayment schedules that would ensure that repayments did not exceed a 'reasonable' percentage of income, for example 10 per cent. Michael McPherson has argued for a reduction in the subsidies paid under the GSL Program, through the interest subsidies to borrowers and the special allowance to lenders. He argues that a persistent problem has been the combining in a single programme elements of loan insurance or guarantee, and loan subsidies which now represent over half the costs of the GSL Program, and therefore force the federal government to ration loans by fixing strict income limits, to restrict eligibility and the size of loans. By reducing these subsidies, so that borrowers paid interest closer to market rates and lenders received a smaller 'special allowance', the federal government would introduce genuine market incentives into the loan programme. At present, McPherson argues:

> The GSL program appears to make extensive use of the attributes of private credit markets but in reality . . . the program has succeeded in

wiping out pretty thoroughly all reliance on market incentives in its operation. Indeed, the main achievement of the program – the widespread availability of guaranteed student loans without regard to credit worthiness of the borrower – has been accomplished largely through this circumvention of the market. (McPherson in Gladieux, 1989, p.18)

A recent study of all Federal Credit programmes in the USA (Bosworth *et al.*, 1987) also argues that the subsidy element of GSLs is now excessive.

> Our evaluation suggests that the student loan program does encourage college enrolments, but that at least 75 per cent of the subsidies go to students who would have attended college without the programme. Thus it has become an expensive way of promoting education. (ibid., p.149)

Bosworth *et al.* also argue that the special allowance has enabled lenders, and practically the secondary market, the Student Loan Marketing Association, or Sallie Mae, to earn high profits on loans which, because of the federal guarantee are practically devoid of credit risk.

One reason why the 'special allowance' was originally thought necessary, was because of high costs of servicing student loans. But Cronin points out that many lenders contract out the servicing of student loans to two huge servicing companies, owned by banks, which are able to reduce the administrative costs, and Bosworth points out that GSLs 'have a guaranteed yield of 3.5 percentage points above the Treasury bill rate, yet loan servicing costs have averaged only about 1.1 per cent of the loan portfolio in recent years' (ibid., p.144).

Such research has led to proposals for a reduction or even elimination of subsidies for loans under the GSL Program, but the problem, as Hauptman recognizes, is that

> Bankers and representatives of other financial institutions that participate in the program have always insisted that they would withdraw from the program if the return to lenders was reduced in any serious way. Because there is so little competition to GSL in the student loan market place, few policy makers appear willing to call the bankers' bluff. (Hauptman in Gladieux, 1989, p.79)

It is not clear what Congress will decide to do, and whether it will opt for radical reform or incremental change, but further changes in student aid can certainly be expected in the United States during the 1990s.

Summary of recent trends and lessons for the United Kingdom
Certain common trends can be observed in the various changes that
have been proposed or introduced in recent years. First, the United
Kingdom is not alone in seeking to shift more of the financial burden
of student maintenance to students and their families. As evidence
accumulates that 'free' higher education, coupled with grants for
student maintenance, do not ensure equality of opportunity, but tend
to benefit upper-income families, several countries have reduced
subsidies for upper-income students, and the recent proposals in
Australia go even further in requiring a substantial contribution to
tuition costs in the interests of equity.

One result of these changes is that in several countries student
support is now targeted more effectively on financially needy students.
In the United States, with eligibility for subsidized loans dependent on
family income, there is now a considerable range of loan programmes,
with different repayment terms. However, as Janet Hansen points out,
this flexibility has resulted in increasing complexity, which it is feared
discourages some low-income and minority students.

Reliance on loans rather than grants has increased in the 1980s,
particularly in the US and the Federal Republic of Germany. Sweden
is unusual in reversing this trend. Loans accounted for 75 per cent of
total student aid when 'study means' was first introduced in 1965, but
by 1987 the proportion was nearly 95 per cent. From 1989 grants, as
well as loans, will be index-linked, and loans will represent 70 per cent
of the total. In introducing loans Britain is therefore following a
widespread trend.

Another significant trend is towards income-contingent rather than
simple mortgage-type loans. Growing concern about high debt
burdens, particularly in the US and Sweden, has led to experiments
with income-contingent loan repayments, which many economists
have advocated as the most equitable form of student loan. Experience
in the US and Sweden shows that some form of low-income insurance
is vital, if default rates are to be kept low. However, it must
be emphasized that even in the US, where default rates have been
widely publicized, over 85 per cent of all graduates do repay their loans
promptly.

The lessons for the UK are clear. A system of student support which
combines grants with loans, preferably with income-contingent
repayments, and with insurance for the unemployed or low paid, is
perfectly feasible, and would be more equitable than a system of grants
that is now increasingly recognized as inadequate.

References

Barr, N. A. and Low, W. (1988), *Student Grants and Student Poverty,* Discussion Paper No 28, Welfare State Programme, London School of Economics.

Bosworth, B. P., Carron, A. S. and Rhyne, E. H. (1987), *The Economics of Federal Credit Programs.* Washington, DC: The Brookings Institution.

College Board (1989), *Up Date from Washington: a report from the Washington Office of the College Board,* February.

Committee on Higher Education Funding (1988), *Report of the Committee on Higher Education Funding* (Chairman: Neville Wran). Canberra: Australian Government Publishing Service.

Council for Industry and Higher Education (1988), *Towards a Partnership: supporting more students.* London: Council for Industry and Higher Education.

Friedman, M. (1962), *Capitalism and Freedom.* Chicago: University of Chicago Press.

Gladieux, L. (ed.) (1989), *Radical Reform or Incremental Change? Student Loan Policy Alternatives for the Federal Government.* New York: College Entrance Examination Board.

Hansen, W. L. (1983) 'Impact of Student financial aid on access' in Froomkin, J. *The Crisis in Higher Education.* New York: TheAcademy of Political Science.

Hawke, G. R. (1988), *Report of the Working Group on Post Compulsory Education and Training* (Convenor: Professor G. R. Hawke). Wellington: Victoria University of Wellington.

Johnstone, D. B. (1986), *Sharing the Costs of Higher Education.* New York: College Entrance Examination Board.

Organization for Economic Co-operation and Development (1988), *Changing Patterns of Finance in Higher Education: Country Study: Japan.* Paris: OECD.

Reuterberg, S-E. and Svensson, A. (1987), 'Student financial aid and participation in Swedish higher education: recruitment effects of student financial aid', *Scandinavian Journal of Educational Research, 31,* 4, 151-161.

World Bank (1986), *Financing Education in Developing Countries: an exploration of policy options*. Washington, DC: World Bank.

Chapter Five
Student Aid in Sweden: Recent Experience and Reforms
Martin Morris

A national system of student financial aid aimed at improving equality of educational opportunity has existed in Sweden since 1918. Such aid was awarded on the basis of high academic merit and was relatively limited in character. It consisted mainly of interest-free loans, but for bright but poor students some rent-free accommodation was available, together with private and local government scholarships. In 1939 some state scholarships were introduced which covered board and lodging during the first two years of study and by 1964 about half the university student population held such scholarships. During the 1950s the loan scheme was expanded, the award of a loan being dependent not only on academic achievement but on the financial status of both the student and his or her parents. Not surprisingly only a minority of students had access to this type of aid. To expand equality of educational opportunity the Swedish goverment decided that improvements to the system of financial aid were needed. In 1959 a national commission was appointed, its remit being the design of a new system of social benefits for students at universities and other institutions of higher education. The recommendations of the commission were accepted by government in 1964 and implemented in 1965. This system remained, with only a few changes, until 1988, when major changes were announced. This chapter outlines the system in 1988, the causes of dissatisfaction and the reforms introduced in January 1989.

The 1988 study-means (studiemedel) system
There are three financial aid programmes in Sweden *(studiehjälp* for upper secondary pupils, *studiemedel* for students in higher education and *studiepenning* for adults taking part-time courses). This chapter

considers only the programmes that serve both full- and part-time students in higher education and school pupils aged twenty or above, the *studiemedel* system. The system is administered by the *Centrala Studiestödsnämnden* (CSN)and the main objectives when established in 1965 were:

1. The expansion of higher education.
2. The elimination of differences in participation rates between men and women and between different socio-economic groups.
3. The provision of a satisfactory standard of living for students during their period of study, in order to ensure completion of studies within a reasonable time.

All higher education students are entitled to study means *(studiemedel)*. The study means programme consists of two parts; a loan component and a grant component. In 1965, when the system was first introduced, the grant component comprised 25 per cent of the total study means; by 1988 this had fallen to 5.8 per cent. The explanation for this is that the total study means available is indexed to the inflation rate, but this is achieved by increasing the loan portion so that the grant as a proportion of the total has gradually declined. The amount of money that a student received is linked to the so-called 'base amount'. It may be noted that there is confusion, even in Sweden, about what this means. It seems that a 'base amount', or sum of money deemed to be required for a pensioner to live on (a subsistence minimum), was established in the 1950s as a feature of a social security policy, and has been increased with time in relation to the level of inflation. Study assistance is calculated as a percentage of this base amount: in 1965 it was 140 per cent and from January 1985, 145 per cent. Requests for additional money are permitted if courses of study are particularly expensive and an additional loan of 25 per cent of the base amount is also available if students have dependent children. The latter is inflation proofed. Table 5.1 shows the relationship between study assistance and the 'base amount' at intervals during the existence of *studiemedel*. The grant began in 1965 as SKr 1,750 (about £145) – 25 per cent of the total study assistance of SKr 7,000 (approximately £583). Although subsequently adjusted twice, the grant has remained at SKr 2,180 (about £200) since 1976.[1]

The total financial aid award is presumably based on what the government perceives to be the needs of the student for a nine months' academic year. For 1988 this was SKr 37,430 (£3466), including the grant of SKr 2,180 (£202) (CSN, 1987). In contrast to the United

States, the United Kingdom and the Federal Republic of Germany, parents are deemed to have no financial responsibility for their children who enter higher education; thus there is no expected parental contribution, nor is there believed, officially, to be any need for part-time work. There are no tuition fees, so that the costs to be borne comprise maintenance, books and equipment.

When applying for assistance students may ask for the grant only, the grant plus the maximum loan, or some lesser amount. Although neither their parents nor their spouses are means-tested, students must state their own income and assets. These declarations can be checked by the CSN fairly easily since in Sweden there is a good database on all citizens and, given the relatively small student population (fewer than 200,000 enrolled in 1985), enforcement of accurate reporting is not a problem (Carlsson, 1988). Study-means was reduced by 50 per cent of the students' own earnings in excess of SKr 30,000/year (£2,778) and by 40 per cent of all assets over SKr 155,000 (£14,352) in the 1987-88 academic year. Payment ceases when income reaches SKr 100,700/ year (£9,324) or when assets reach SKr 242,000 (£22,407).

Study assistance is available for both full-time and part-time courses, is usually available for six academic years, and can normally be paid until the student has reached the age of forty-five. In practice the upper age limit occasionally exceeds this. The first time a student registers for higher education, study assistance is given without any aptitude test being conducted. For study assistance to continue, however, the student must demonstrate acceptable progress which, for most courses, means passing a minimum of 75 per cent of the course taken, by the end of the third term (halfway through the second year). Should the student fail to achieve this by virtue of illness or other special circumstances then this is taken into account.

Government expenditure on study assistance for students in higher education in 1987-88 was SKr 3,100 million on loans (£287 million) and SKr 20.1 million on grants (£18.6 million). The total budget for 1987-88 for all programmes was SKr 7,977 million (£738.6 million) which included an administration cost of SKr 124 million (£11.48 million). The cost of administration at approximately 1.6 per cent of the total budget seems remarkably low when compared for example, with Canada (4.5 per cent) (Woodhall, 1982). Income from loan repayments was SKr 1,300 million (£120.4 million). From Table 5.2, which itemizes the total CSN budget for 1987-88, it may be calculated that about 41 per cent of expenditure on study assistance was devoted to higher education.

Table 5.1. The Increase in the Base Amount, Study Assistance and Child Allowance during the Period 1965-88

Year	Base amount		Study assistance		Child allowance	
	SKr	£	SKr	£	SKr	£
1965	5,000	417	7,000	583	1,250	104
1970	6,300	525	8,820	735	1,250	131
1975	9,000	900	12,600	1,260	2,250	225
1980	15,400	1,571	21,560	2,200	3,850	393
1985	21,800	2,180	31,626	3,163	5,454	545
1988	25,820	2,391	37,341	3,457	6,455	597

Note: The sums relate to a nine-month academic period.
SKr = Swedish crowns

Between 1965 and 1988 the exhange rate fluctuated considerably. In this table the average rate of exchange in each year has been used; this varies between £1 = SKr 9.8 in 1980 to £1 = SKr 12 in 1965.
Source: Johansson and Ricknell, 1986 (modified).

Table 5.2. The Total Budget for Student Financial Assistance 1987-88

Programme	Grants (millions)		Loans (millions)	
	SKr	£	SKr	£
Studiehjälp	2046	189.4	63	5.8
Upper secondary				
Studiemedel				
Higher education	201	18.6	3100	287.0
Upper secondary	68	6.3	980	90.7
Studiepenning				
Short-cycle courses	200	18.5	–	–
Long-cycle courses	741	68.6	169	15.6
Other				
Hourly compensation	166	15.4		
Visiting work places	51	4.7		
Subsidized rail travel	68	6.3		
Sub-totals	3541 (a)	327.9	4312 (b)	399.3
Adminstration	124 (c)	11.5		
TOTAL (a)+(b)+(c)	7977	738.6		
Income (loan repayments)	1300	120.4		

Note: In the above calculations the exchange rate £1 = SKr10.8 has been used.
During the period of this study the exchange rate fluctuated between £1 = SKr 10.45 and £1 = SKr 11.2.

Source: CSN.

Repayment terms (1988)

Repayment period
There is a two-year 'grace period' before repayment of a loan must commence. Borrowers aged up to thirty-six have until their fifty-first birthday in which to repay, and those aged between thirty-six and fifty-one have a fifteen-year repayment period. Small debts have to be paid in a shorter time. Repayments are made in June, September and December.

Annual repayment sum
The total debt divided by the number of years for repayment

determines the portion to be repaid in the first year. After that repayment is increased annually by 4.2 per cent, the annual adjustment index, which is equivalent to a rate of interest. In 1988 the minimum repayment was SKr 2,580 (£239).

Deferment and cancellation
Deferment of payment is permitted when income is less than SKr 90,300 (£8,361) for a borrower without children and less than SKr 116.000 (£10,740) for a borrower with children. Deferments obviously lead to an extended repayment period. Remaining debt is cancelled in the event of death, permanent disability and on attaining the age of sixty-six. Cancellation of SKr 5,700 (£528) of the amount borrowed to study in upper secondary school may be made for adults who attended such a school in order to qualify for entry to higher education. Table 5.3 shows the repayment plan for a student with a twenty-year repayment period and a debt of SKr 40,000 (£3,704).

In 1978 there was a total of 501,000 study loans; in 1984 this figure was 795,000 and in 1988 it was 910,000, with 682,000 making repayments (Carlsson, 1988). The difference between these last two figures is made up of those who are still studying and those who have completed their studies but are still within the two-year 'grace period'.

Default
About 5 per cent of borrowers are subject to 'collecting measures' and about 80 per cent of this problem group reside in Sweden. Failure to pay an instalment produces a reminder, in the form of an invoice, from CSN, and if there is no response to this, either by payment or application for deferment, then a second invoice is sent. If this is ineffective then the matter is put in the hands of the Crown Bailiff who has recourse to the law to enforce payment. Defaulting students living in Norway, Finland and Great Britain are now contacted by a private debt-collecting agency and this has led to a great increase in the recovery of payments (Carlsson, 1988). The proportion of genuine defaulters has been reduced to about 1 per cent of borrowers.

The hidden grant
While the grant portion of *studiemedel* is an overt subsidy there is a second effective subsidy or 'hidden grant', by virtue of charging an interest rate on the loan portion, which, at 4.2 per cent is considerably below commercial rates of interest (commonly 11 per cent in 1987-88). If it is assumed that 10 per cent approximates the true commercial rate of interest on a loan of SKr 1,000, that is, 10 per cent is deemed to be

Table 5.3 Repayment Plan for a Student with a Twenty-Year Repayment Period and Debt of SKr 40,000 (£3,704) in 1984.

Year	Debt at 1 January	Repayment Charge	Debt after repay't	Index 4.2%	Debt at 31 December
1	40,000	2,000	38,000	+1,596	39,596
2	39,596	2,084	37,512	1,576	39,088
3	39,088	2,172	36,916	1,550	38,466
4	38,466	2,263	36,203	1,521	37,724
5	37,724	2,358	35,366	1,485	36,851
6	36,851	2,457	34,394	1,445	35,839
7	35,839	2,560	33,279	1,398	34,677
8	34,677	2,668	32,009	1,344	33,353
9	33,353	2,780	30,573	1,284	31,857
10	31,857	2,897	28,960	1,216	30,716
11	30,176	3,019	27,157	1,141	28,298
12	28,298	3,146	25,152	1,056	26,208
13	26,208	3,278	22,930	963	23,893
14	23,893	3,416	20,477	860	21,337
15	21,337	3,559	17,778	747	18,525
16	18,525	3,708	14,817	622	15,439
17	15,439	3,864	11,575	486	12,061
18	12,061	4,026	8,035	337	8,372
19	8,372	4,195	4,177	175	4,352
20	4,352	4,352	0	0	0
Total		60,802		20,802	

Source: Johansson and Ricknell (1986), p.61.

the appropriate discount rate, then, given a repayment period of 20 years, the loan has a present value of SKr 472. Thus the student is receiving an effective or 'hidden' grant of SKr 528 (52.8 per cent) and the 'true loan' is SKr 472 (Johnstone, 1986). Together with the true grant element (5.8 per cent) the total state subsidy amounts to approximately 59 per cent.

Evaluation of the study means system
In evaluating the Swedish *studiemedel* system attention has been focused on the objectives of the system when it was first introduced. However, factors other than financial aid, which may have a bearing on the achievement of those objectives, have also been considered.

Transition rates, participation by different socio-economic groups and completion rates
Reuterberg and Svensson of the Department of Education, Gothenberg University, have conducted a series of investigations into the effects of study assistance on participation in higher education (see references below). They began by studying a nationally representative sample of those born in 1948, and these individuals were classified according to the education and occupation of their father. Five groups were distinguished, namely:

A. academics, senior civil servants and industrialists
B. civil servants and white-collar workers having had a higher education
C. white-collar workers without a higher education
D. farmers
E. labourers

(It should be noted that different research workers distinguish socio-economic groups in different ways. A more frequently used categorization is as follows:

Group I   parents are white-collar workers, with post secondary school education and in high positions.
Group II   parents are white-collar workers with or without post-secondary education, in lower positions than Group I.
Group III parents are blue-collar workers.)

It may be calculated from the data of Reuterberg and Svensson

(1983,p.19) that while those in group A comprised only 5 per cent of the sample, 58 per cent had entered higher education by the age of 23, and of these 54 per cent had successfully completed their studies by the age of 26. By contrast, those in group E comprised 50 per cent of the total but only 9 per cent had entered higher education by the age of 23 and of these 39 per cent had successfully completed their studies by the age of 26. Thus, a clear relationship between social background and higher education was shown to exist. Given the aims of the student financial assistance these figures were startling, and provoked Reuterberg and Svensson to question whether the system of financial aid had made any contribution at all to equalizing opportunity for higher education. Their questionnaire in 1980 to students making up the sample therefore posed the question:

If there had been no financial aid available when you entered higher education, would you have begun to study at all?

Yes, definitely . . . .( )
Yes, probably . . . .( )
No, probably not . . . .( )
No, definitely not . . . . ( )

From the replies it became clear that financial aid had exerted a positive effect, since 26 per cent of respondents indicated that they would probably not have entered higher education without aid and this was true for both sexes. The proportion was greatest amongst students on open admission programmes in arts and sciences. Further, the aid was shown to have been particularly important for those from the lower socio-economic groups (Table 5.4). The researchers were aware that some students, because of the availability of financial aid, may

Table 5.4. Socially Equalizing Effects of Student Financial Aid on a Cohort born in 1948

Socio-economic group	Would not have entered higher education without aid (%)	Completing degrees who would not have entered higher education without aid (%)
A + B	12	6
C	27	20
D + E	40	24

Source: Reuterberg and Svensson (1983). Reprinted by permission of Kluwer Academic Publishers.

have been lured into an educational programme which they were not able to complete. However, this appeared not to be the case, completion rates being similar for those who would and those who would not have entered without financial aid. Table 5.4 also demonstrates the socially equalizing effects of financial aid in terms of the proportion of students from different socio-economic groups completing a degree programme.

A comparison between this 1948 cohort and a cohort born in 1953 has been made (Reuterberg, 1986), in terms of the influence of student aid on their transition to, or participation in, higher education. Since the questionnaires were given to the cohorts in 1983 when individuals were aged about thirty, both cohorts judged the benefits of aid retrospectively. From the study Reuterberg concluded that:

1. Utilization of study assistance was practically independent of social background and sex.
2. The probability of entering a degree course was five times greater for those from the higher socio-economic strata than those from the lower strata.
3. When compared with the influence of social background, sex and intelligence, study assistance had the greatest effect on probability of completion.
4. Study assistance was of greatest effect on probability of completion amongst students from lower social strata.

Although there was generally a positive reponse to study assistance, some negative aspects were noted namely:

1. The probability of degree completion had decreased.
2. There was a decreasing influence of study assistance on the probability of degree completion among students in open admission courses.

These observations prompted the author to pose the question: are these tendencies the effects of changes in the study assistance system, or are they the result of changes in other factors? Reuterberg concluded that the increasingly difficult situation in the labour market was the main causative factor, many students in the second cohort tending to opt for a job before completing a degree. This trait was most prevalent in the open admission faculties (arts and sciences) for whose graduates employment prospects were poorest. Poor employment prospects have also increased the tendency for students to enter university who do not intend completing their course. Many of these are students who would normally have studied part-time and who formerly (before *studiemedel*) would not have qualified for aid.

More recently a third sample of individuals born in 1948 and 1953 (Reuterberg and Svensson, 1986; Reuterberg and Svensson, 1987a and 1987b). The following major points emerged:

1. Overall transition rate from secondary to post-secondary education has continued to decline.
2. The difference in transition rate between the higher and lower socio-economic groups has remained virtually unchanged throughout the period.
3. During the late 1970s and early 1980s women have increasingly participated in higher education, so that the transition rate for them by 1980 was higher than for men.
4. The significance of achievement at upper secondary school has increased and for the 1963 cohort became the most important determinant of participation rates.

The increasing influence of achievement on participation rate in higher education can be explained by the fact that the open admissions policy to certain courses, particularly within the faculties of arts and sciences, has been modified in response to the introduction of restrictions in intake to higher education. Hence more competition for places has meant that selection on the basis of achievement has increased. While this may be one cause of the decline in transition rate, such a decline was greatly in evidence before the introduction of new admission rules; and furthermore, the transition rate has declined among students of high achievement. By way of explanation Reuterberg and Svensson (1986) comment that: 'the labour market for people who have a university education has deteriorated considerably. Therefore, many young people have refrained from higher education'. Particular difficulty with gaining employment has been experienced by those who entered faculties of arts and social sciences and these programmes are mostly chosen by students from the lower social strata.

Reuterberg and Svensson also examined the effect of financial aid on recruitment to higher education. When questioned as to whether or not they would have entered higher education in the absence of financial aid those who replied 'definitely not' or 'probably not' were deemed to have been recruited by the student financial aid system. This suggested that the recruitment effect of financial aid was considerable, for students entering higher education in 1968, but it

declined in the 1970s, and rose very slightly in the 1980s. Summing up
these results, Reuterberg and Svensson (1987b) observe: 'at the
beginning of this period (of study means) the aid had a significant
socially equalizing effect, an effect which has now been lost'.

Similarly, a recent review by the CSN (1988) concludes:

> Higher education recruitment has changed a great deal during the 20
> years that have passed since the study assistance scheme was introduced.
> The student population has virtually doubled . . . study assistance had
> been very much a precondition of this expansion. Surveys have shown
> that almost 40 per cent of students would not have embarked on their
> studies if study assistance had not existed. For students from the lower
> classes, the figure is 50 per cent. But the socially equalizing effect of study
> assistance appears to have come to a standstill in recent years. (CSN,
> 1988, p.17)

Participation by women
Within the 1948 and 1953 cohorts there was only a marginal increase in
the transition rate for women. However, the authors concluded that
the financial aid system had achieved some equalizing effect on sex
differences in choice of programme (Reuterberg and Svensson, 1983).
In particular it had increased the entry of women into closed admission
programmes such as medicine and dentistry where men are greatly in
the majority. Within the 1963 cohort (entering higher education in
1983-86) the participation rate for women was higher than for men,
and Reuterberg and Svensson (1986) conclude that this is due to
student financial aid. This trend had in fact begun much earlier. For
example in the autumn of 1980 of the 153,280 students registering,
some 54.7 per cent were women (Abrahamsson, 1987) and by 1985 56
per cent of undergraduates and 30 per cent of postgraduates were
women (data from the Swedish Embassy, London).

Participation by older students
One striking change in Swedish higher education in the 1970s and
1980s has been the increase in the proportion of older students, which
is partly the result of the 1977 reform of higher education and the
introduction of the 25/5 rule (later to become the 25/4 rule) whereby
those aged 25 or above and with five (or four) years' work experience
can qualify for entry to higher education if they so wish. A second
reason for the increase in average age of students is that due to changes
in demand in the labour market many adults have embarked on
retraining programmes. This means that the age profile of students has
shifted upwards, and while the transition rate from upper secondary to

higher education has declined, as Reuterberg and Svensson have shown, the participation of older students (above the age of 25) has increased. Figure 5.1 shows the marked change in the age distribution of students in higher education during the 1970s and the 1980s. By concentrating on the declining transition of young secondary school leavers to higher education, at a time when adult participation was increasing, Reuterberg and Svensson may have painted a more gloomy picture of overall participation in higher education in Sweden than is strictly warranted, if participation by both young people and mature students is taken into account.

Figure 5.1. Students in higher education by age.

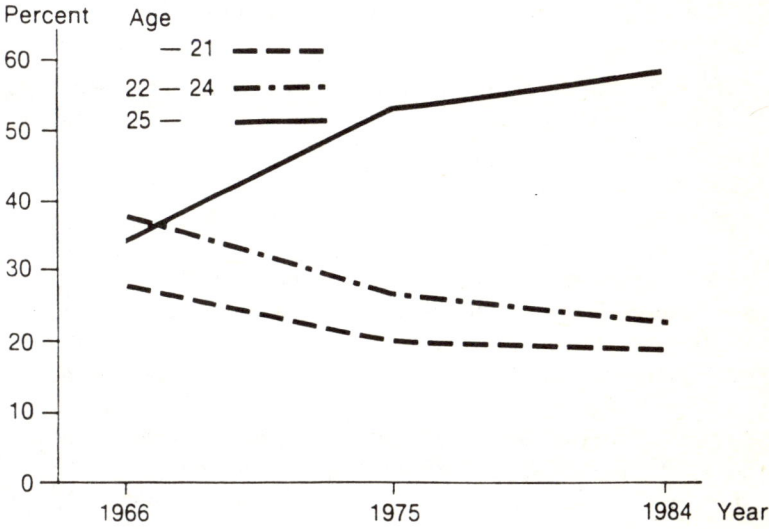

Source: CSN (1988)

Adequacy of financial aid

In the survey of the 1948 cohort by Reuterberg and Svensson, only 20 per cent of men and 33 per cent of women stated that it was possible to finance their students entirely from *studiemedel*. Given that one of the intentions of this financial aid programme was that the awards to students should cover all the costs of living during an academic year these proportions are very low. One obvious explanation for this is that increases in the size of the awards have not kept pace with inflation. Thus students have relied on parental contributions and earnings from part-time work in order to meet necessary expenses. A less obvious explanation might be that, because students have recieved help from their parents and increased thier incomes through part-time work they have been able to enjoy a better standard of living than was strictly necessary. Consequently they have underestimated the importance and adequacy of financial aid through *studiemedel*. This issue underlies the view expressed by the governments of several countries, namely that students tend to confuse 'wants' with 'needs'.

In reporting the results of the survey of a cohort born in 1963 Svensson (1987) noted that those who had not begun post-secondary studies in 1983, and did not plan to do so, usually quoted two reasons:

1. Concern about future debts (62 per cent of respondents).
2. Difficulty in living on the amount of financial aid which was available (57 per cent).

Both obstacles were listed most frequently by those students coming from socio-economic groups II (white collar workers in low positions) and III (blue-collar workers).

The increasing proportion of mature students, noted above, also helps to explain why many students regard the level of aid as inadequate. Figure 5.1 showed more than half of all students in higher education are now over 25. Mature students may well be married and have children. Consequently their expenses, and hence their income requirements, are greater than those of young, single students. The *studiemedel* system was originally designed for students below the age of 25 and living with their parents. Olsson (1988b) believes that the current level of financial aid is still acceptable to those living with parents but is inadequate for those living on their own.

During the 1980s there has been a reduction in the number of small flats available in Sweden due apparently to the merging of these to create larger ones as part of the process of modernization. The demand for flats is greatest in the expanding regions of Sweden where a number of the universities are to be found and therefore students face grave difficulties in finding accommodation. In his paper on student housing in Sweden, Hultman (1987) reported that some 446,000 persons were on a waiting list for a flat and that 138,000 of them were under the age of 25. Some are likely to remain on the waiting list for a long time since in 1986 the total number of flats supplied by the municipal housing authority was 103,000 and a large proportion of those on the waiting list are seeking a flat for single occupancy.

A recent survey (SIFO, 1983) reported that 21 per cent of students had accommodation in student rooms or flats; 53 per cent lived in private flats or houses; 11 per cent lived with their parents; 13 per cent were boarders. Thus the majority of students have to find accommodation in competition with everyone else. The demand by students for flats or accommodation of their own is understandable, given that 60 per cent of them are over 25 years of age and 30 per cent over 30 years old. While a government housing grant is available for young people under the age of 28, this is not extended to students.

Rental costs vary greatly; student accommodation is relatively inexpensive (for example a single room in Stockholm costs an average SKr 868 per month (£80) and SKr 598 per month (£55) in Umeå, northern Sweden. The 53 per cent of students competing for rooms on the open market can expect to pay SKr 1,200 per month (£111.00) for one room in Stockholm and SKr 850 per month (£79) in Umeå. The cost of all forms of accommodation has risen more than the average rate of inflation during the 1980s and more than various consumer price-indices. Those students living long distances from universities and colleges are likely to form the majority faced by this problem. As Svenson (1987) has shown, those who live furthest from the major centres of education generally come from the lower socio-economic strata, the target group for financial aid!

The decline in study assistance to a level where it has become unattractive has been documented by Nilsson (1988). He has expressed the maximum study means available as a proportion of the average salary of clerks in industry, aged 20-24, during the first twenty years of the *studiemedel* system. Throughout the 1960s the maximum study means award stood at 60-62 per cent of average salaries for industrial clerks, but in the 1970s this proportion declined to reach a nadir in 1977 of 45 per cent (Figure 5.2). This coincides with the decline in participation in higher education. Improvements in the level of the loans portion of study aid in the 1980s meant that it compared more favourably with the average earnings of industrial clerks but nevertheless, in 1985, the maximum study means was still only 53 per cent of the average wage of clerks. This latter improvement may well be the explanation for the observation by Reuterberg and Svensson (1987b) that in the 1980s study assistance had partially countered the decline in the transition from upper secondary to higher education.

Debt levels
Studiemedel is largely composed of a repayable loan element (94.2 per cent in 1987), because this portion of the financial assistance package

has been index-linked and the grant portion has not. In the late 1970s and early 1980s high inflation had the effect of rapidly increasing the loan portion and, thereby, greatly increasing the level of student indebtedness. For example a student attending a three-year degree course and receiving maximum *studiemedel* for the whole course will incur a total debt of SKr 130,000 (£12,000) by the time that repayment commences. Even when compared with the United States, this level of indebtedness is high and is very high when compared with that in European countries. Of those who commenced repayment in 1988 approximately 14 per cent owed more than SKr 100,000 (£9,260) and this proportion will increase as those currently in higher education complete their studies. One law student at Stockholm University estimated that she would borrow between SKr 150,000 and SKr 200,000 (£13,800 – £18,500) during her four and a half year course.

As graduate salaries are not high compared with non-graduate salaries repayment problems are likely to increase. The most vulnerable group are probably the mature students who have received study loans during both their upper secondary and university periods.

Figure 5.2. Studiemedel expressed as a proportion of the Average Earnings of Industrial Clerks aged 20-24

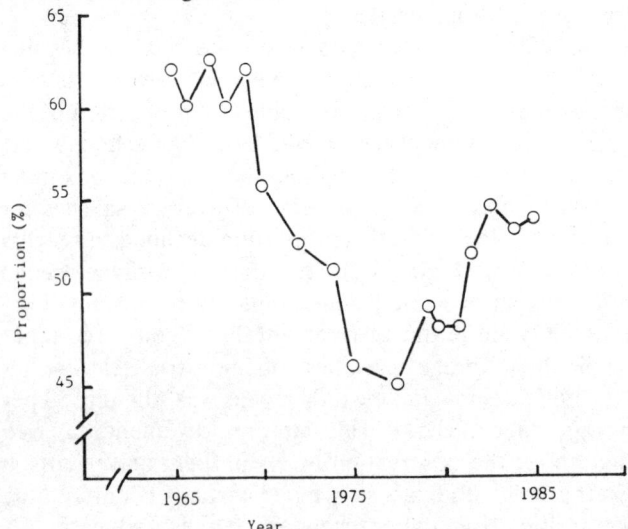

Note: For the years 1965-69 the group used for comparison was aged 20-23 and because average earnings would thus have been lower this partly accounts for the higher proportion values for this period.

Source: Based on Nilsson (1988)

Studiemedel and higher education as a private investment
Though many factors influence the decision to participate in higher education in Sweden financial considerations are particularly important for both young people and adults in the lower socio-economic groups. These considerations include not only job opportunities and salary levels on graduation, but also study assistance, when assessing the likely profitability of attending a particular course or obtaining a particular qualification. Ideally therefore, study-aid should enable the student to meet all academic costs, without incurring such a burden of debt that repayments would make the private rate of return unattractive. Such an objective has implications for both the size of the loan and the terms of repayment.

Unlike the United Kingdom, graduate salaries in Sweden are not high when compared with non-graduate salaries. Has investment in higher education during the period of *studiemedel*, therefore, led to satisfactory pecuniary benefits?

Figure 5.3 taken from Nilsson (1988), shows the differences in expected life-time earnings after tax deductions of some university educated professionals compared with bank clerks. While the expected life-time earnings for the librarian have always been less than for the bank clerk, those for the assistant master and the dentist exceeded those for the bank clerk in the 1960s and the early 1970s but subsequently these professions could not expect higher life-time earnings than a clerk. The holder of the economics/accountancy degree can still anticipate greater life-time earnings than the bank clerk although the projection for such graduates in 1985 is only 50 per cent of that in 1960.

This erosion of the earnings differential is reflected in the private rate of return estimates. Figure 5.4 shows, for example, the decline in the private rate of return for a civil engineer who will have spent six years in higher education (Nilsson, 1988).

A rate of return of 10 per cent in the late 1960s has become one of only 1.5 per cent by the mid-1980s. However, there will be those who may look upon this with envy: the assistant master's investment in higher education now produces a slightly *negative* rate of return and that of the librarian a return of perhaps -5 per cent (Carlsson, 1988). By contrast, the university-trained engineer in Britain can expect a private rate of return of 14-18 per cent, even when the maintenance grant is excluded (Clark and Tarsh, 1987). Even the medical profession in Sweden saw a real income decline by 40 per cent in the late 1960s and early 1980s, and a similar decline in income for those in the legal profession is believed to be the cause of the current shortages in that profession (Olsson, 1988a).

Figure 5.3. Differences in Expected Life Income after Tax for some University Educated Professions compared with Bank Clerks

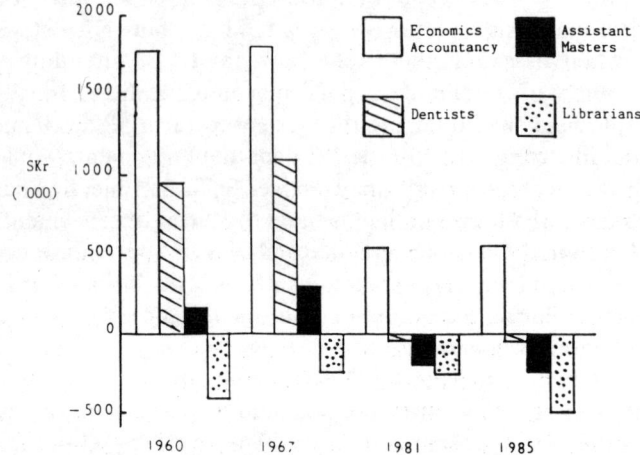

Source: Based on Nilsson, (1988)

Figure 5.4. Private Rate of Return for a Civil Engineer having spent Six Years in Higher Education (compared with non-university trained engineers).

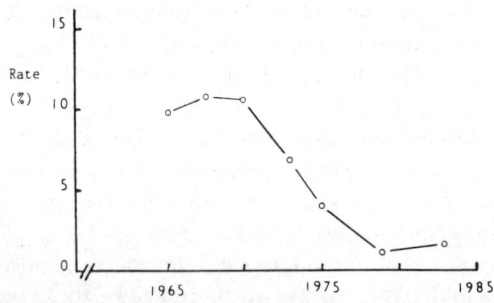

Source: Based on Nilsson, (1988)

Summary of conclusions about the 1988 system of study assistance
While, as intended, study assistance facilitated the expansion of higher education in the late 1960s, the transition rate from secondary to higher education has subsequently declined sharply. Increases in the level of study assistance in the 1980s only partially arrested this decline.

Initially, study assistance had a socially equalizing effect on entry to higher education, but became increasingly less influential in this respect and the equalizing effect has now been lost, so that the social composition of the student body today is essentially the same as it was before the introduction of *studiemedel*.

Study means has been instrumental in increasing the participation of women in higher education. This appears to be a persistent effect.

The employment prospects for graduates have deteriorated and salary differentials between graduates and non-graduates have been eroded during the 1970s and 1980s to the extent that higher education has become a poor investment. For some professions negative rates of return are forecast. Those graduating from the open faculties have been most badly affected, and these are people who tend to come from the lower socio-economic groups.

There has been an increase in the proportion of older students, but many of these find the level of study means inadequate.

The level of study assistance has become inadequate as a result of high inflation in the late 1970s and early 1980s. Rising costs of accommodation, food and books, all of which have exceeded the average level of inflation, mean that students have been particularly disadvantaged.

Because the grant portion of study-means has been fixed and the loan portion indexed to inflation the loan portion has increased from an initial 75 per cent of the total in 1965 to 94.2 per cent in 1988 with consequent increase in the indebtedness of students.

Study assistance has had a decreasing influence on the frequency of degree completion, particularly in open admission faculties.

These findings lead to the conclusion that the *studiemedel* system has been undermined by the recession in the economy in the late 1970s and early 1980s.

Apart from increasing the participation by women in higher education, the *studiemedel* system appears not to have achieved the initial objectives; transition by young people to higher education continues to decline; there has been no long-term socially equalizing impact on entry to higher education; frequency of degree completion is in decline; and the level of study means does not permit a reasonable living standard for the 53 per cent of students who live in private accommodation away from home.

Partly as a result of such criticisms, by the CSN and Swedish Students Union, the Swedish government set up a national commission in 1985 to reappraise the *studiemedel* system. Their report, submitted in the autumn of 1987, led to parliamentary approval in the spring of 1988 for a revised system.

The revised studiemedel system

In an attempt to redress the deficiencies previously outlined, as from January 1989, a revised system comes into effect. The changes to be implemented are:

1. The total amount of study means will be raised by 17 per cent.
2. The grant portion will be 50 per cent of the 1988 'base amount' and will thus increase as a proportion of study means from 5.8 per cent to 30 per cent. Further, the grant is to be index-linked. This change is aimed at attracting students from socio-economic Group III (Olsson 1988a).
3. The loan amount is to be reduced but the increase in grant will mean that the total financial aid will become 170 per cent of the 'base amount' instead of the current 145 per cent.
4. The child-supplement loan is abolished and since child benefits are available from other welfare sources this will have the effect of reducing the level of debt for the many students with children (the CSN felt that the child allowance was, in any case, too generous).
5. Reductions for earnings will begin with the grant. If earnings are such as to expunge the grant, the loan will then be reduced as required. Reducing study means because of assets such as a house is abolished since it is considered unreasonable to expect students to liquidize such an asset in order to finance their higher education; a more practical reason is that very few students have assets in excess of SKr 155,000 (£14,350) the current threshold at which reductions begin.
6. Since the grant portion has been increased and the loans portion reduced, the repayment terms are now more strict. The 'grace period' is reduced from two years to six months and the interest is to be 50 per cent of the current rate on government loans (probably 5½ – 6½ per cent). Interest payments will not be tax-deductable.
7. The annual repayment sum will be 4 per cent of gross income earned two years previously. Since incomes will vary, no repayment period can be specified. Income contingent repayment should reduce the repayment burden on persons in low income jobs with heavy educational debts.
8. Deferment of repayment will still be possible and debts will be cancelled at 66 years of age or in the event of death or permanent disability.

9. To help the vulnerable mature student who borrows to finance both upper secondary and higher education, one-third of the debt incurred in the upper secondary school will be cancelled if he or she subsequently completes three terms in higher education. This change, in effect, introduces an incentive into the system to encourage those embarking on retraining programmes.

The old and the new systems are compared in Table 5.5.

Some observations on the revised system

A particularly noteworthy change in the system is the shift in subsidy, from the interest payable on the loan, to the grant. Thus the 'hidden grant' element has been reduced while the increase in subsidy through the grant means that students benefit when their needs are greatest. As a trade-off for increasing the level of grant and making it inflation-proof the repayment terms have been made more exacting through an increase in interest rate on the loan and a reduction in the length of 'grace period'.

A minor criticism of the new system is that as earnings-related reductions in the size of study means begin with the grant portion, those who seek to avoid a large loan (or even avoid a loan) by taking part-time work are consequently penalized. The counter argument might be: firstly, since this rule may discourage part-time work it could have the effect of improving efficiency by stimulating student throughput and production of graduates, and secondly, since both the grant and loan elements are now inflation-proofed there should, as was the original intention in 1965, be no need for part-time work.

Table 5.5. Comparison between the 1988 and revised (1989) studiemedel system

(£1.00 = SKr 10.8)	1988 System		System from 1.1.89	
	SKr	£	SKr	£
Grant	2,180	202	12,900	1,194
Loan	35,250	3,264	30,960	2,867
Total	37,430	3,466	43,860	4,061
Child supplement	6,460	598	abolished	
Reductions				
Income	50% of income over		50% of income over	
	30,000	2,778	34,000	3,148
Assets	40% of assets over		abolished	
	155,000	14,352		

(Table 5.5 continued)

	1988 System	System from 1.1.89
Repayment terms		
Interest	4.2%	50% of interest on Government loans, plus small addition for administrative costs.
'Grace period'	2 years	0.5 year

Repayment period	Start	Period	
	aged 36	until aged 51	No specified period as is income contingent
	aged 36-51	15 years	
	aged 51+	until aged 66	
	small debts, shorter time extended time after deferment.		

Annual repayment	Total debt divided by the number of years determine the instalment in first year. Increases each year by 4.2%	4% of income
Minimum repayment	In 1988 SKr, 2,580 (£239)	4% of income (i.e. gross income 2 years previously)
Deferment	Allowed when income is lower than SKr 90,300 (£8,361) for borrower without children. SKr 116,000 (£10,740) for borrower with children	Allowed if the borrower takes part in further courses. Reduced charges in hardship cases.
Cancellation	Remaining debt at 66 in case of death permanent disability Certain groups: at most SKr, 5,700 (£528) of debt incurred in upper secondary schooling	Remaining debt at 66 in case of death permanent disability Certain groups: ⅓ of debt incurred in upper secondary schooling

Despite the reduction in the loan portion, increase in the grant portion, and resultant increase in the total amount of study means, the share of the costs borne by the student may be little different from the share under the old system because of the changes in repayment terms, particularly the increase in interest charges. Certainly, with the shift of subsidy to the grant portion, the system appears more benign than the previous one, but if the net effect is that there will be no change in the proportion of student-borne costs, then the revised system will make no impact on the private rate of return to higher education. Both the CSN and the Ministry of Education and Cultural Affairs would almost certainly argue that an improvement in the salaries of university educated professionals is the answer to this problem. This must surely be the case; without this it is difficult to envisage the revised *studiemedel* system having much impact on participation in higher education particularly by those from the lower socio-economic groups. A greater impact on the latter would probably have been secured by making student financial assistance more selective. However, in Sweden there appears to be determined political resistance to such an approach.

Note

1. Between 1965 and 1988 the exchange rate fluctuated between £1 = SKr 12 and £1 = SKr 9.8. The exchange rate of £1 = SKr 10.8 (the average for 1988) is used throughout this chapter, except for the historical figures when the average for that year has been used.

References

Abrahamson, K. (1987), *Adult participation in Swedish Higher Education*. Stockholm: Almqvist & Wiksell International.

Carlsson, L. (1988), Interview with Leif Carlsson at CSN, Sundsval, Sweden, 19 May.

Clark, A. and Tarsh, J. (1987), 'How much is a degree worth?' *Education and Training, UK*. London: Policy Journals, pp. 109-115.

CSN (1987), 'Studiemedelsbelopp', *Centralastudiestödsnämnden informationsektioen.* Sundsval, Sweden: Centrala Studiestödsnämnden.

CSN (1988), *Study Assistance in Sweden*. Sundsval, Sweden: Centrala Studiestödsnämnden.

Hultman, R. (1987) 'Student housing in Sweden', Student housing seminar, Trinity College, Dublin. 3-6 September. West European Student Information Bureau (WESIB).

Johansson, O. and Ricknell, L. (1986), *Study Assistance in Ten European Countries: overview and conceptual framework.* Study assistance project: Research report. Sweden: University of Umeå.

Johnstone, D. B. (1986), *Sharing the Costs of Higher Education: student financial assistance in the United Kingdom, the Federal Republic of Germany, France, Sweden and the United States.* New York: College Entrance Examination Board.

Nilsson, A. (1988), 'Studeranderekrytering och studerandeekonomi 1965 – 1985 med en utblick mot år 2000' in N.–O. Christofferson et al., *Det omöjliga systemet.* Stockholm: Sveriges Förenade Studentkårer.

Olsson, W. (1988a) Interview with Mr Billy Olsson, Director CSN, Sundsval, Sweden, 19 May.

Olsson, W. (1988b) 'The student financial aid system in Sweden'. Paper presented to the Student Aid Conference, Reykjavik, Iceland, April.

Reuterberg, S-E. (1986), 'Study assistance and degree completion in Swedish higher education', *Studies in Higher Education, 11*, 2, 155-171.

Reuterberg, S-E. and Svensson, A. (1983), 'The importance of financial aid; the case of higher education in Sweden', *Higher Education, 12*, 89-100.

Reuterberg, S-E and Svensson, A. (1986), 'Student financial aid and participation in higher education: changes between 1965 and 1985 in Sweden'. Paper presented to American Education Research Association annual meeting.

Reuterberg, S-E. and Svensson, A. (1987a) 'Student financial aid and participation in Swedish higher education: 1. The effects of background variables on transition to higher education'.*Scandinavian Journal of Educational Research, 31*, 4, 139 – 150.

Reuterberg, S-E. and Svensson, A. (1987b) 'Student financial aid and participation in Swedish higher education: 2. Recruitment effects of student financial aid'. *Scandinavian Journal of Educational Research, 31,* 4, 151-161.

SIFO (1983), *Vuxensturderande-ekonomi, studier och arbete* (adult students, economy, studies and work). Stockholm: Svensk Institutet för Opinionen.

Svensson, A. (1987), 'Financial aid and higher education' in K. Abrahamsson (ed.), *Implementing Recurrent Education in Sweden: reform strategies of Swedish adult and higher education.* Stockholm: Swedish National Board of Education.

Woodhall, M. (1982), *Student Loans: lessons from international experience.* London: Policy Studies Institute.

Chapter Six
Alternative Proposals for Student Loans in the United Kingdom
Nicholas Barr

This chapter[1] starts with an analysis of the current grant system, and proceeds to a discussion of different types of loan. A specific loan scheme is advocated in the final section.

Problems with the grant system
The UK system of financing students by way of grants looks less rosy today than in the first flush of the Robbins expansion. Even then it attracted criticism because it relied on the parental contribution to top up the grant. No government, however, has been willing to implement the recommendation of the Anderson Committee (Ministry of Education/Scottish Education Department, 1960) that grants should be wholly state financed. The grant today is even further from providing full maintenance (Barr and Low, 1988; Moore and Roberts, 1988), even when the parental contribution is included. The Department of Education and Science admitted to the Select Committee on Education that 'we would no longer maintain that the maintenance element of the mandatory award is sufficient to meet all the essential expenditure of the average student' (*The Times*, 3 December 1986, p.5).

Many students do not receive even this reduced amount, however. In 1982-83 40 per cent of students received less in grant and parental contribution than they should according to the grant system. The average shortfall for each student in deficit was about 14 per cent of the full grant. Even when income from all sources (e.g. including the student's earnings) is taken into account, one student in eight received less than the grant system says he or she should.

Thus the grant system, judged in its own terms, does not perform very well. As a result, even taking all sources of income into account,

110

one student in 13 in 1982-83 was below the long-term supplementary benefit level. There is no reason to believe that this situation has changed for the better, rather the contrary. The main reason for these deficits (and in itself another problem with the grant system) is the failure of the parental contribution system. Of those students who should have received a parental contribution only half received the full amount; the remainder received on average only £53 of every £100 of assesssed contribution (Barr and Low, 1988 pp.31-36).

The deficiencies in the parental contribution system render it universally unpopular, contribute to poverty among students and deter an unknown number from applying in the first place. In addition, there is solid anecdotal evidence of students with a substantial shortfall in parental contributions working long hours to earn money, at the expense of the quality of their degree. This is inefficient, in that it distorts the division between studying and earning which a student would choose with a larger grant or in the presence of a sensible loan system.

Though students are often poor their parents are not, since the majority of students come from middle-class backgrounds. A further problem with the system, therefore, is that it disproportionately benefits students from better-off families. Compared with the population at large, students are twice as likely to come from higher-income families (the top 40 per cent of incomes), and over three times as likely to come from those with the highest incomes (roughly the top 12½ per cent of incomes). Students at Oxford and Cambridge are 2½ times as likely to come from a higher income family, and nearly four times as likely to come from one in the highest income ranges (Barr and Low, 1988, pp.49-59).

Finally, the grant system is expensive, making it difficult to expand the higher education system. Thus the UK has relatively few students; in the United States, Japan and the Federal Republic of Germany, for instance, between two and three times as many people from the relevant age group go to university.

Alternative systems of student loans
It is possible (Hills, 1988; Hills and Kelly, 1988) to link student loans and student finance of higher education in a logical and coherent structure. There are strong attractions to doing so, but it is important to be clear that the two issues are separable. Loans can be combined with the present system of university finance and its prospective successor. Equally, the government could fund students in whole or in

part without resorting to loans, but university fees could be raised to economic levels.

The loans strategy

A partial switch to loans could increase efficiency in at least three ways. First, higher education benefits society as a whole, and it therefore aids the efficient allocation of resources if the state pays part of the cost. However, a degree also confers private benefits on students (higher pay, greater job satisfaction), and so it is both efficient and equitable if students pay part of the cost themselves.

Second, is the issue of capital markets. If capital markets were perfect (i.e. if all students could borrow against their future earnings) the private market could supply loans itself. Since many students are not able to obtain long-term private loans, government intervention is necessary, either to guarantee private loans or to provide loans itself.

Third, loans reduce the public costs of higher education, making it easier to expand the system to a larger and (it can be argued) more efficient size.

Loans, additionally, can have equity advantages. They reverse the tendency of the grant system disproportionately to benefit the better off. They reduce the public cost of higher education and so would make it easier to pay grants to 16-18 year olds, which is where the main bottleneck occurs in the progress of children from poorer backgrounds towards higher education. Finally, it would be possible to replace parental contributions by a loan system, a desirable objective, given all their problems. It is desirable also because the idea of taxing the parents of academically successful children is bizarre; it makes much more sense to give the children access to their own future earnings and then later to tax the *children*.

Debate about loans has been bedevilled by confusion over different types of scheme. The distinction between *commercial loans* (which may or may not have a subsidized interest rate) and *income-related loans* (where repayment is based on a student's subsequent income) cannot be over-emphasized. Critics of loans invariably attack the former, as though no other way of organizing loans existed. This section argues that loans with income-related repayments are the productive way forward.

Commercial loans

Commercial loans resemble a mortgage. Repayment is related to the size of the loan, to the interest rate and to the speed with which the loan is repaid. There are major arguments against commercial loans as the primary source of undergraduate finance (though, in many cases, it may be the more useful approach for graduate study).

The first problem is practical. Many students would not be able to obtain a long-term loan from a bank or building society. The apparent solution is for the government to offer a loan guarantee, thus increasing the amount of money in students' pockets without raising public spending. This line of argument is a mirage for a least three reasons. The first is purely technical: Treasury rules require the *whole* of the guaranteed sum to be added to public expenditure.

Second, even if the rule were relaxed, commercial loans would still involve considerable public spending. Financial markets for student loans do not work well; doing a degree, for the reasons discussed shortly, is risky; in addition, there is no collateral (slavery being illegal). Thus banks will not be prepared to offer large, long-term loans to students without a Treasury subsidy on interest rates (extra public spending) and a Treasury guarantee. Given the degree of riskiness, the Treasury guarantee will not be a mere fiction, but will be costly (in the US the default rate is currently running at about 14 per cent of outstanding loans, and a total deficit of approaching $5 billion).

Third, because of the cost of subsidies and loan guarantees, the Treasury will impose stringent controls on the total amount of loan guaranteed. There will be a battle every time it is proposed to raise the amount a student can borrow or to extend the range of students eligible. The point is acutely relevant to those currently in receipt of non-mandatory awards, whose size and number have been constricted by pressures on local revenues. Second qualifications and further professional training are usually financed by such awards, and there is a strong case for helping mature students and those in need of retraining. In sum, it is a myth to assume that commercial loans do not involve added public spending. They are costly and on that account the system is not readily extensible.

An additional, and fundamental, problem arises on the demand side. Commercial loans are inefficient: they waste talent if they deter able but impoverished young people from embarking on higher education; they reduce inter-generational mobility; and they may create artificial scarcities in certain occupations resulting in surges in pay. Furthermore, they do nothing to eliminate the parental contribution.

It is sometimes pointed out that people from the lower socio-economic groups will take out a mortgage to buy a house, so why would they not borrow to buy a degree? The analogy is wholly inapplicable. In addition to the tax advantages for house purchase, when someone buys a house (a) he knows what he is buying (because he has lived in a house all his life), (b) the house is unlikely to fall down, and (c) he has a fairly good idea that the value of the house is likely to appreciate. When someone borrows to buy a degree (a) he is not fully certain what he is buying (particularly if from a family with no degree holders), (b) there is a high risk (or at least a perceived high risk) of failing the degree outright, and (c) not all degrees are going to be rewarded as expected over a lifetime, because fashions and employment prospects can change. For all these reasons borrowing to buy a degree is considerably more risky than borrowing to buy a house, and the risks are likely to be greater for those from a poorer background and for women.

Commercial loans have other problems. The default rate, as discussed earlier, is likely to be substantial. In addition, they are unpopular for a least two reasons with the banks who would have to operate them. First, they will be costly to administer. Second, students have threatened to boycott commmercial banks which participate in a government loan scheme. In the past, banks could shrug off such threats. Now that building societies have joined the clearing system, however, banks fear an exodus of student accounts to building societies.

Income-related loans

Loans with income-related repayments organized, for instance, via the tax system once a student has finished his or her degree, are automatically related to ability to pay[2]. Such loans have major advantages. Students pay part of the cost of their degree themselves, which is both efficient and fair. The scheme resolves the worst problems of capital imperfections. In the long run (though not necessarily in the short run) the public cost of expanding higher education is reduced. The scheme limits the extent to which the better-off benefit most from the grant system. It solves the problem of unpaid parental contributions, thereby improving access to higher education for those people (often women or mature students) whose parents do not pay the assessed amount. In the long run the approach could increase equality of opportunity by using saved public spending to finance grants to 16-18 year olds. In short, such a scheme would make access to higher education easier for students from poor backgrounds. For these and other reasons

virtually every advocate of student loans in Britain (Alan Peacock, Jack Wiseman, Alan Prest, Sir Charles Carter, Gareth Williams, Ernest

> Rudd, Anthony Flew, Donald Mackay, Michael Crew, Alistair Young, Arthur Seldon, Lord Robbins, and Mark Blaug) . . . favours an income-related loans scheme . . . and not a personal loan repayable in a fixed number of years after taking up employment. (Blaug, 1980, p.45)

The choice of repayment model has relevance not only to a student's access to higher education but also to his or her subsequent career. Harvard Law School has an income-related loan scheme which enables its graduates to go into community service, an option largely foreclosed by the need to repay a large commercial loan. Income-related repayments are thus arguably more efficient (given a world which departs from the competitive ideal), in that they distort job choices less than commercial loans.

Not least because of these advantages a number of such schemes exist or are under discussion. The Swedish government introduced a scheme in 1966 by the simple expedient of freezing the grant. Fees continued to be publicly funded for all students, and the grant was topped up by a loan from the state, with repayments related to subsequent income, and with additional assistance for students from disadvantaged backgrounds. A scheme to be introduced in Australia on 1 January 1989 will recoup part of the cost of higher education by imposing an additional one per cent income tax on graduates with above average earnings, rising to 3 per cent for those on the highest incomes.

The present government, it is fair to say, has not made distributional goals its primary objective. It has, however, stressed fairness and independence; and a better-educated workforce is likely to raise national wealth. Helping people to progress educationally accords with both objectives: commercial loans do little to help; loans with income-related repayments make a considerable contribution. They should be adopted for two reasons: they foster intergenerational mobility; and they give people training (cf, the various job training schemes).

National Insurance based loan scheme[3]
This section advocates a specific loan scheme with repayments related to a student's subsequent income, which can be phased in without even the short-run necessity for an increase in public spending. Though the idea of income-related loans is old, the mechanism suggested here is new.

The idea

Repayments should be based on earnings rather than a student's total income (which includes investment income), because it is earnings which are increased by having a degree, and also because it would be an administrative nightmare to withhold tax on investment income at a different rate for graduates than for others. Repayments should also be finite. If they were (say) 2 per cent of taxable income for life, Mick Jagger (one and a bit years as an LSE undergraduate) could end up financing more or less the whole system of UK student support. Repayment can be limited by paying a percentage of all earnings until the loan is paid off, or by paying for life, but only on a band of income.

A natural way of meeting both requirements is for students to take out loans from the state, and to make repayments in the form of a graduate addition to the National Insurance Contribution (NIC). This, it turns out, is feasible for quite a modest increase in NICs.

What is more, for a given student population, the scheme can be introduced without the necessity for any increase in public spending. The starting point is to set the level of next year's grant in the usual way, and initially to keep in place the system of parental contributions. In addition, announce two changes: that henceforth 10 per cent of the grant, the percentage rising over time, will be repayable via an addition to NICs; and that the parental contribution will be phased out as rising repayments make it possible to do so without increasing public spending. The system thus costs the same as current arrangements for about three years, at which point repayment revenues start to come in.

Arithmetic

The arithmetic of the scheme suggests that it is feasible for a relatively small increase in NICs. Table 6.1 shows the extra contribution to repay a £1,000 loan under different assumptions. With a 5 per cent interest rate, for example, an individual with national average earnings can repay a £1,000 loan over 25 years with an additional NIC of 0.6 pence per pound, i.e. by paying contributions at 9.6 per cent of earnings rather than the current rate of 9 per cent.

It is plausible to assume that most graduates will have at least national average earnings over the course of their working lives. Suppose, for simplicity, that the grant is £2,500. At a 5 per cent interest rate, half the grant for a three year degree could be repaid over 25 years by an additional NIC of 2¾ pence per pound of earnings. At a 7½ per cent interest rate (roughly the mortgage rate after tax) the extra NIC would be 2¾ per cent. It would thus be possible to abolish parental contributions (which average almost half the full grant) at no public cost with an extra NIC of around 2½ per cent of earnings for the typical student. If graduates command salaries at or above the upper earnings limit, half the grant could be repaid at an interest rate of 7½ per cent by a 2 per cent additional contribution.

Table 6.1 *Additional National Insurance Contribution (pence per £1) for each £1000 borrowed*[a]

	10 years	15 years	20 years	25 years
5% interest rate				
£6000[b] per year	2.11	1.57	1.31	1.16
£11,648[c] per year	1.09	0.81	0.67	0.60
£15,860[d] per year	0.80	0.59	0.49	0.44
7½% interest rate				
£6000[b] per year	2.35	1.83	1.58	1.45
£11,648[c] per year	1.21	0.94	0.81	0.74
£15,860[d] per year	0.89	0.69	0.60	0.55
10% interest rate				
£6000[b] per year	2.60	2.10	1.87	1.76
£11,648[c] per year	1.34	1.08	0.97	0.90
£15,860[d] per year	0.98	0.79	0.71	0.66

NOTES: [a] Per £1000 borrowed; compound, monthly repayments
[b] £6000 = approximately half of national average earnings
[c] £11,648 = national average earnings
[d] £15,860 = upper earnings limit for national insurance contributions

There are other possibilities. The extra contribution could be paid until the loan has been paid off or for life: the former relates contribution more strictly to benefit, the latter is more redistributive. Either is defensible: neither raises administrative problems. It would also be possible to share the additional cost between employer and employee, not least to economize on skilled personnel in the context of a declining number of young people. If repayment were over the whole working life, half the grant could be replaced by an extra NIC of 1 per cent each for employee and employer, i.e. a 'penny in the pound' scheme.

In the longer term, once the system is well-established, it could be extended to cover a large proportion of the grant. Assuming national average earnings, a 5 per cent interest rate and repayment over 25 years, the entire grant could be replaced by an additional NIC of 2¼ per cent of earnings each for employer and employee. The maximum annual repayment (for someone at the upper earnings limit) would be just over £350 per year, with a similar payment by the employer. Someone earning £6,000 per year would repay £11.25 per month. Readers can make their own assumptions and use the figures in Table 6.1 to devise their own scheme.

Advantages
The scheme has very major advantages over the current system and also over the various loan schemes already considered. The inefficient and highly unpopular parental contribution could be phased out; the phasing out can be achieved without any increase in public spending; and the process could be accelerated as public expenditure constraints permitted, if the government so wished.

There are other advantages. Since the student benefits from having a degree, it is right that he or she should contribute towards its costs; and, like any loan scheme, the one suggested here reduces the extent to which students from better-off families benefit disproportionately from the grant system. Furthermore, repayments based on national insurance are related to the student's subsequent income. Someone who is unemployed makes no repayments whilst he or she is unemployed; and a graduate nurse pays back very little, at least early in her career. Both features are crucial to the efficiency and equity, and also to the political acceptability, of any substantial reliance on loans.

The scheme causes no major administrative problems. All students have a National Insurance number already or could easily obtain one. The scheme requires no separate legislation, but only the insertion of the relevant clauses into the Finance Bill. Furthermore, the scheme would be cheap to implement and bad debts would be minimal. Individuals have neither the opportunity to evade NICs on any substantial scale nor, importantly, any incentive to do so, since evasion affects future benefit entitlement. Since the additional contribution is small, it is unlikely *per se* to cause emigration; and in the unlikely event that emigration caused problems, government (except for students who emigrate upon graduation) has the individual's past contributions and his/her future benefits as security.

The use of NICs has additional advantages when compared with repayments via the income tax system, of the sort incorporated in the new Australian scheme. Unlike income tax, repayments via NICs are based on earnings but, appropriately, not on investment income. They also solve the 'Mick Jagger' problem referred to earlier; for those above the upper earnings limit the additional NIC is equivalent to a lump sum tax, with the important efficiency advantage that it will not distort the choice between jobs. Repayments are levied on an individual basis, and so there is no problem of husbands being asked to repay the loans of non-working graduate wives; thus they solve automatically the so-called 'negative dowry' problem. They also lend themselves readily to an employer contribution.

It has been suggested in a British context that the Inland Revenue is very reluctant to administer a scheme based on income tax. In contrast, the national insurance mechanism is absolutely the right vehicle for repayments. The former student is paying for part of his or her degree, and so repayment properly takes the form of a contribution, which is an important aspect of national insurance. People already pay contributions for a future benefit like pensions; here they pay a contribution for a past benefit. The principle is entirely the same: in both cases national insurance enables an individual to redistribute income over his or her lifetime. The resulting system is also a form of group insurance: the risk of borrowing to finance a degree is taken on by the generation of graduates as a whole, rather than by individual students, who are protected against unemployment and other contingencies. Since there are technical problems with private insurance for risks like unemployment (Barr, 1987, Chapter 8), it is *efficient* as well as equitable for the state to organize student loans in this way.

The government should implement a scheme along these lines as a matter of urgency.

Notes

1. This chapter is taken from: Barnes, J. and Barr, N. (1988), *Strategies for Higher Education: the alternative White Paper*. Aberdeen University Press. It is reprinted here by kind permission of Aberdeen University Press.

2. The first explicit proposal in a British context was by Prest (1966); see also Blaug (1966), Glennerster, Merrett and Wilson (1968) and Robbins' (1980, pp.31-7) account of his conversion to loans. The literature is surveyed by Blaug (1970) and systems elsewhere discussed by Woodhall (1978), Blaug and Woodhall (1979). For more recent discussion see Glennerster (1981) and Farmer and Barrell (1982)

3. The section is based, almost in its entirety, on ideas suggested to us by Mervyn King.

References

Barr, N. A. (1987), *The Economics of the Welfare State.* London: Weidenfeld & Nicolson.

Barr, N. A. and Low, W. (1988), *Student Grants and Student Poverty,* Discussion Paper No.28, Welfare State Programme, London School of Economics.

Blaug, M. (1966), 'Loans for students?', *New Society,* 6 October, 538-539.

Blaug, M. (1967), 'Approaches to educational planning', *Economic Journal,* June.

Blaug, M. (1970), *An Introduction to the Economics of Education.* Harmondsworth: Penguin.

Blaug, M. (1980), 'Student loans and the NUS', *Economic Affairs,* October, 45-56.

Blaug, M. (1987), *The Economics of Education and the Education of an Economist.* Aldershot: Edward Elgar.

Blaug, M. and Woodhall, M. (1979), 'Patterns to subsidies to higher education in Europe', *Higher Education,* September, 331-363, reprinted in Blaug (1987).

Farmer, M. and Barrell, R. (1982), 'Why student loans are fairer than grants', *Public Money,* **2,** 1, 19-24.

Glennerster, H. (1981), 'Role of the state in financing recurrent education: lessons from European experience', in M. Bowman, (ed.), *Collective Choice in Education,* United States: Kluwer – Nijhoff.

Glennerster, H., Merrett, S. and Wilson, G. (1968), 'A graduate tax', *Higher Education Review,* Vol. **1,** No. 1.

Hills, G. (1988), 'Education for the enterprising', *Scottish Enterprise Culture: a Radical Reaffirmation,* Cooper and Lybrand Gleneagles Conference.

Hills, G. and Kelly, A. (1988), 'An alternative funding scheme for higher education', submission to the Committee of Vice-Chancellors and Principals Working Group on the Finance of Higher Education.

Ministry of Education/Scottish Education Department (1960), *Grants to Students* (the Anderson Report), Report of the Committee Appointed by the Minister of Education and the Secretary of State for Scotland, Cmnd 1051, London, HMSO.

Moore, A. and Roberts, G. (1988), *A Consumer's Guide to Student Finance.* London: Telegraph Publications.

Prest, A. R. (1966), *Financing University Education.* London: Institute for Economic Affairs.

Robbins, L. C. (1980), *Higher Education Revisited,* Basingstoke: Macmillan.

Woodhall, M. (1978), *Review of Student Support Schemes in Selected OECD Countries.* Paris: Organization for Economic Co-operation and Development.

Index

Bedford Way Series

ISSN 0261-0078